THE CHALDEAN ACCOUNT OF GENESIS,
CONTAINING THE DESCRIPTION OF THE CREATION,
THE FALL OF MAN, THE DELUGE, THE TOWER OF
BABEL, THE TIMES OF THE PATRIARCHS, AND
NIMROD:
BABYLONIAN FABLES, AND LEGENDS OF THE GODS;
FROM THE CUNEIFORM INSCRIPTIONS.

TABLE OF CONTENTS

INTRODUCTION.

SOME explanation is necessary in introducing my present work. Little time has elapsed since I discovered the most important of these inscriptions, and in the intervening period I have had, amidst other work, to collect the various fragments of the legends, copy, compare, and translate, altering my matter from time to time, as new fragments turned up. Even now I have gone to press with one of the fragments of the last tablet of the Izdubar series omitted.

The present condition of the legends and their recent discovery alike forbid me to call this anything more than a provisional work; but there was so general a desire to see the translations that I have published them, hoping my readers will take them with the same reserve with which I have given them.

I have avoided some of the most important comparisons and conclusions with respect to Genesis, as my desire was first to obtain the recognition of the evidence without prejudice.

The chronological notes in the book are one of its weak points, but I may safely say that I have placed the various dates as low as I fairly could, considering the evidence, and I have aimed to do this rather than to establish any system of chronology.

I believe that time will show the Babylonian traditions of Genesis to be invaluable for the light they will throw on the Pentateuch, but at present there are so many blanks in the evidence that positive conclusions on several points are impossible. I may add in conclusion that my present work is intended as a popular account, and I have introduced only so much explanation as seems necessary for the proper understanding of the subject. I have added translations of some parts of the legends which I avoided in my last work, desiring here to satisfy the wish to see them as perfect as possible; there still remain however some passages which I have omitted, but these are of small extent and obscure.

October 26, 1875.

CHAPTER I: THE DISCOVERY OF THE GENESIS LEGENDS.

Cosmogony of Berosus.—Discovery of Cuneiform Inscriptions.—
Historical texts.—Babylonian origin of Assyrian literature.—
Mythological tablets.—Discovery of Deluge texts.—Izdubar, his
exploits.—Mutilated condition of tablets.—Lecture on Deluge
tablets."—Daily Telegraph" offer.—Expedition to Assyria.—-
Fragments of Creation tablets.—Solar Myth.—Second journey to
Assyria.—Tower of Babel.—Clay records.—Account of creation in
"Telegraph."—"Daily Telegraph" collection.—Interest of Creation
legends.—The Fall.—New fragments.—List of texts.

THE fragments of the Chaldean historian, Berosus, preserved in the works of various later writers, have shown that the Babylonians were acquainted with traditions referring to the Creation, the period before the Flood, the Deluge, and other matters forming parts of Genesis.

Berosus, however, who recorded these events, lived in the time of Alexander the Great and his successors, somewhere about B.C. 330 to 260; and, as this was three hundred years after the Jews were carried captive to Babylon, his works did not prove that these traditions were in Babylonia before the Jewish captivity, and could not afford testimony in favour of the great antiquity of these legends.

On the discovery and decipherment of the cuneiform inscriptions, Oriental scholars hoped that copies of the Babylonian histories and traditions would one day be discovered, and we should thus gain earlier and more satisfactory evidence as to these primitive histories.

In the mound of Kouyunjik, opposite the town of Mosul, Mr. Layard discovered part of the Royal Assyrian library, and further collections, also forming parts of this library, have been subsequently found by Mr. H. Rassam, Mr. Loftus, and myself. Sir Henry Rawlinson, who made the preliminary examination of Mr. Layard's treasures, and who was the first to recognize their value, estimated the number of these fragments of inscriptions at over twenty thousand.

The attention of decipherers was in the first instance drawn to the later historical inscriptions, particularly to those of the Assyrian kings contemporary with the Hebrew monarchy; and in this section of inscriptions a very large number of texts of great importance rewarded the toil of Assyrian scholars. Inscriptions of Tiglath Pileser, Shalmaneser, Sargon, Sennacherib, Esarhaddon, Nebuchadnezzar, Nabonidus, and numerous other ancient sovereigns, bearing directly on the Bible, and giving new light upon parts of ancient history before obscure, for a long time occupied almost exclusively the attention of students, and overshadowed any work in other divisions of Assyrian literature.

Although it was known that Assyria borrowed its civilization and written characters from Babylonia, yet, as the Assyrian nation was mostly hostile to the southern and older kingdom, it could not be guessed beforehand that the peculiar national traditions of Babylonia would be transported to Assyria.

Under these circumstances, for some years after the cuneiform inscriptions were first deciphered, nothing was looked for or discovered bearing upon the events of Genesis; but, as new texts were brought into notice, it became evident that the Assyrians copied their literature largely from Babylonian sources, and it appeared likely that search among the fragments of Assyrian inscriptions would yield traces at least of some of these ancient Babylonian legends.

Attention was early drawn to these points by Sir Henry Rawlinson, who pointed out several coincidences between the geography of Babylonia and the account of Eden in Genesis, arid suggested the great probability that the accounts in Genesis had a Babylonian origin.

When at work preparing the fourth volume of Cuneiform Inscriptions, I noticed references to the Creation in a tablet numbered K 63 in the Museum collection, and allusions in other tablets to similar legends; I therefore set about searching through the collection, which I had previously selected under the head of "Mythological tablets," to find, if possible, some of these legends. This mythological collection was one of six divisions into which I had parted the Museum collection of cuneiform inscriptions for convenience of working. By placing all the tablets and fragments of the same class together, I had been able to complete several texts, to easily find any subject required, and at any time to get a general idea of the contents of the collection.

The mythological division contained all tablets relating to the mythology, and all the legends in which the gods took a leading part, together with prayers and similar subjects.

Commencing a steady search among these fragments, I soon found half of a curious tablet which had evidently contained originally six columns of text; two of these (the third and fourth) were still nearly perfect; two others (the second and fifth) were imperfect, about half remaining, while the remaining columns (the first and sixth) were entirely lost. On looking down the third column, my eye caught the statement that the ship rested on the mountains of Nizir, followed by the account of the sending forth of the dove, and its finding no resting-place and returning. I saw at once that I had here discovered a portion at least of the Chaldean account of the Deluge. I then proceeded to read through the document, and found it was in the form of a speech from the hero of the Deluge to a person whose name appeared to be Izdubar. I recollected a legend belonging to the same hero Izdubar K. 231, which, on comparison, proved to belong to the same series, and then I commenced a search for any missing portions of the tablets.

This search was a long and heavy work, for there were thousands of fragments to go over, and, while on the one side I had gained as yet only two fragments of the Izdubar legends to judge from, on the other hand, the unsorted fragments were so small, and contained so little of the subject, that it was extremely difficult to ascertain their meaning. My search, however, proved successful. I found a fragment of another copy of the Deluge, containing again the sending forth of the birds, and gradually collected several other portions of this tablet, fitting them in one after another until I had completed the greater part of the second column. Portions of a third copy next turned up, which, when joined together, completed a considerable part of the first and sixth columns. I now had the account of the Deluge in the state in which I published it at the meeting of the Society of Biblical Archaeology, December 3rd, 1872. I had discovered that the Izdubar series contained at least twelve tablets, and I afterwards found this to be their exact number. Of this series the tablet describing the Deluge was the eleventh and K 231, the sixth. Numerous other fragments turned up at the same time; but these, while they increased my knowledge of the legends, could not be arranged in order from want of indication of the particular tablets to which they belonged.

Some other fragmentary legends, including the war of the gods and three fables, I also found at the same time, but these were in such mutilated condition that I could not make a connected translation of them.

In my lecture on the Deluge tablets, I gave a sketch of the Izdubar legends, and expressed my belief that the Chaldean inscriptions contained various other similar stories bearing upon the Book of Genesis, which would prove of the highest interest.

Just at this time happened the intervention of the proprietors of the "Daily Telegraph" newspaper. Mr. E. Arnold, who is on the direction of that paper, had already sent to me expressing his interest in these discoveries, and immediately after my lecture he came armed with a proposition from the proprietors of the "Daily Telegraph" to re-open, at their cost, the excavations in Assyria, and gain some new information on the subject of these legends. This proposition was submitted to the trustees of the British Museum, and they directed me to go to Assyria and make a short excavation, leave of absence for six months being granted to me for this purpose. I have related, in my work, "Assyrian discoveries," the history of this expedition, which brought me the next fragments of these legends. Soon after I commenced excavating at Kouyunjik, on the site of the palace of Assurbanipal, I found a new fragment of the Chaldean account of the Deluge belonging to the first column of the tablet, relating the command to build and fill the ark, and nearly filling up the most considerable blank in the story. Some other fragments, which I found afterwards, still further completed this tablet, which was already the most perfect one in the Izdubar series. The trench in which I found the fragment in question must have passed very near the place where the Assyrians kept a series of inscriptions belonging to the early history of the world. Soon after I discovered the fragment of the Deluge tablet, I came upon a fragment of the sixth tablet of the same series in this trench, and not far from the place of the Deluge fragment. This fragment described the destruction of the bull of Ishtar by Izdubar and Heabani, an incident often depicted on early Babylonian gems. My next discovery here was a fragment evidently belonging to the creation of the world; this was the upper corner of a tablet, and gave a fragmentary account of the creation of animals. Further on in this trench I discovered two other portions of this legend, one giving the Creation and fall of man; the other having part of the war between the gods and evil spirits. At that time I did not recognize the importance of these fragments, excepting the one with the account of the creation of animals, and, as I had immediately afterwards to return to England, I made no further discoveries in this direction.

On my return from the east, I published some of the discoveries I had made, and I now found, on joining the fragments of the Deluge or Izdubar series, that they formed exactly twelve tablets. The fact that these legends covered twelve tablets led to the impression that they were a form of the solar myth, that is, that they symbolized the passage of the sun through the heavens, each tablet representing a separate sign of the zodiac. This opinion, first started by Sir Henry Rawlinson, was at once accepted by M. Lenormant, Rev. A. H. Sayce, and other scholars; but I think myself it rests on too insecure a basis to be true. In a subsequent chapter I will give as nearly as I can the contents of the Izdubar legends, which I think do not warrant this view. Some months further passed, during which I was engaged in my second journey to Assyria, and in realizing the results of that expedition. I again brought from Assyria several fragments of the Genesis legends which helped to complete these curious stories, and in January, 1875, I commenced once more a regular search for these fragments. Very soon afterwards I succeeded in discovering a notice of the building of the tower of Babel, which at once attracted attention, and a notice of it, which appeared in the "Athenæum," No. 2468, was copied into several of the papers. I was, however, at that time hardly prepared to publish these legends, as I had not ascertained how far they could be completed from our present collections.

Subsequent search did not show that any further fragments of the Babel tablet were in the British Museum, but I soon added several fresh portions to the fragmentary history of the Creation and Fall. The greatest difficulty with which I had to contend in all these researches was the extremely mutilated and deficient condition in which the tablets were found. There can be no doubt that, if the inscriptions were perfect, they would present very little difficulty to the translator.

The reason why these legends are in so many fragments, and the different parts so scattered, may be explained from the nature of the material of which the tablets are composed, and the changes undergone by them since they were written. These tablets were composed of fine clay and were inscribed with cuneiform characters while in a soft state; they were then baked in a furnace until hard, and afterwards transferred to the library. These texts appear to have been broken up when Nineveh was destroyed, and many of them were cracked and scorched by the heat at the burning of the palace. Subsequently the ruins were turned over in search of treasure, and the tablets still further broken; and then, to complete their ruin, the rain, every spring soaking through the ground, saturates them with water containing chemicals, and these chemicals form crystals in every available crack. The growth of the crystals further splits the tablets, some of them being literally shivered.

Some idea of the mutilated condition of the Assyrian tablets, and of the work of restoring a single text, will be gained from the engraving below, which exhibits the present appearance of one of the Deluge tablets. In this tablet there are sixteen fragments. The clay records of the Assyrians are by these means so broken up, that they are in some cases divided into over one hundred fragments; and it is only by collecting and joining together the various fragments that these ancient texts can be restored. Many of the old fragmentary tablets which have been twenty years in the British Museum have been added to considerably by fragments which I found during my two journeys, and yet there remain at least 20,000 fragments buried in the ruins without the recovery of which it is impossible to complete these valuable Assyrian inscriptions.

Being now urged by many friends who were interested in the subject, I sent the following account to the editor of the "Daily Telegraph," which was printed in that paper on the 4th of March, 1875:—

"Having recently made a series of important discoveries relating to the Book of Genesis, among some remarkable texts, which form part of the collection presented to the British Museum by the proprietors of 'The Daily Telegraph,' I venture once more to bring Assyrian subjects before your readers.

"In my lecture on the Chaldean Account of the Deluge, which I delivered on Dec. 3, 1872, I stated my conviction that all the earlier narratives of Genesis would receive new light from the inscriptions so long buried in the Chaldean and Assyrian mounds; but I little thought at that time that I was so near to finding most of them.

"My lecture, as your readers know, was soon followed by the proposal of your proprietors and the organizing of 'The Daily Telegraph' expedition to Assyria. When excavating at Kouyunjik during that expedition, I discovered the missing portion of the first column of the Deluge tablet, an account of which I sent home; and in the same trench I subsequently found the fragment which I afterwards recognized as part of the Chaldean story of the Creation, which relic I have noticed already in your columns. I excavated later on, while still working under your auspices, another portion belonging to this story, far more precious—in fact, I think, to the general public, the most interesting and remarkable cuneiform tablet yet discovered. This turns out to contain the story of man's original innocence, of the temptation, and of the fall. I was, when I found it, on the eve of departing, and had not time to properly examine my great prize. I only copied the two or three first lines, which (as I had then no idea of the general subject of the tablet) did not appear very valuable, and I forthwith packed it in the box for transport to England, where it arrived safely, and was presented by the proprietors of 'The Daily Telegraph,' with the rest of their collection, to the British Museum. On my return to England I made some other discoveries among my store, and in the pursuit of these this fragment was overlooked. I subsequently went a second time to Assyria, and returned to England in June, 1874; but I had no leisure to look again at those particular legends until the end of January in this year. Then, starting with the fragment of the Creation in 'The Daily Telegraph' collection, which I had first noticed, I began to collect other portions of the series, and among these I soon found the overlooked fragment which I had excavated at Kouyunjik, the first lines of which I took down in the note-book of my first expedition. I subsequently found several smaller pieces in the old Museum collection, and all join or form parts of a continuous series of legends, giving the history of the world from the Creation down to some period after the Fall of Man. Linked with these, I found also other series of legends on primitive history, including the story of the building of the Tower of Babel and of the Confusion of Tongues.

"The first series, which I may call 'The Story of the Creation and Fall,' when complete must have consisted of nine or ten tablets at least, and the history upon it is much longer and fuller than the corresponding account in the Book of Genesis. With respect to these Genesis narratives a furious strife has existed for many years; every word has been scanned by eager scholars, and every possible meaning which the various passages could bear has been suggested; while the age and authenticity of the narratives have been discussed on all sides. In particular, it may be said that the account of the fall of man, the heritage of all Christian countries, has been the centre of this controversy, for it is one of the pivots on which the Christian religion turns. The world-wide importance of these subjects will therefore give the newly discovered inscriptions, and especially the one relating to the Fall, an unparalleled value, and I am glad, indeed, that such a treasure should have resulted from your expedition.

"Whatever the primitive account may have been from which the earlier part of the Book of Genesis was copied, it is evident that the brief narration given in the Pentateuch omits a number of incidents and explanations—for instance, as to the origin of evil, the fall of the angels, the wickedness of the serpent, &c. Such points as these are included in the Cuneiform narrative; but of course I can say little about them until I prepare full translations of the legends.

"The narrative on the Assyrian tablets commences with a description of the period before the world was created, when there existed a chaos or confusion. The desolate and empty state of the universe and the generation by chaos of monsters are vividly given. The chaos is presided over by a female power named Tisalat and Tiamat, corresponding to the Thalatth of Berosus; but, as it proceeds, the Assyrian account agrees rather with the Bible than with the short account from Berosus. We are told, in the inscriptions, of the fall of the celestial being who appears to correspond to Satan. In his ambition he raises his hand against the sanctuary of the God of heaven, and the description of him is really magnificent. He is represented riding in a chariot through celestial space, surrounded by the storms, with the lightning playing before him, and wielding a thunderbolt as a weapon.

"This rebellion leads to a war in heaven and the conquest of the powers of evil, the gods in due course creating the universe in stages, as in the Mosaic narrative, surveying each step of the work and pronouncing it good. The divine work culminates in the creation of man, who is made upright and free from evil, and endowed by the gods with the noble faculty of speech.

"The Deity then delivers a long address to the newly created being, instructing him in all his duties and privileges, and pointing out the glory of his state. But this condition of blessing does not last long before man, yielding to temptation, falls; and the Deity then pronounces upon him a terrible curse, invoking on his head all the evils which have since afflicted humanity. These last details are, as I have before stated, upon the fragment which I excavated during my first journey to Assyria, and the discovery of this single relic in my opinion increases many times over the value of 'The Daily Telegraph' collection.

"I have at present recovered no more of the story, and am not yet in a position to give the full translations and details; but I hope during the spring to find time to search over the collection of smaller fragments of tablets, and to light upon any smaller parts of the legends which may have escaped me. There will arise, besides, a number of important questions as to the date and origin of the legends, their comparison with the Biblical narrative, and as to how far they may supplement the Mosaic account."

This will serve to exhibit the appearance these legends presented to me soon after I discovered them.

On comparing this account with the translations and notes I have given in this book, it will be evident that my first notice was inaccurate in several points, both as to the order and translation of the legends; but I had not expected it to be otherwise, for there had not been time to collect and translate the fragments, and, until that was done, no satisfactory account of them could be given, the inaccuracies in the account being due to the broken state of the tablets and my recent knowledge of them. It is a notable fact that the discovery of these legends was one of the fruits of the expedition organized by the proprietors of the "Daily Telegraph," and these legends and the Deluge fragments form the most valuable results of that expedition.

After I had published this notice in the "Daily Telegraph" I set to work to look over the fragments in the collection, in search of other minor fragments, and found several, but these added little to my knowledge, only enabling me to correct my notice. A little later I discovered a new fragment of the tenth tablet of the Deluge series, and last of all a further portion of the sixth tablet of these legends. This closed my discoveries so far as the fragments of the tablets were concerned, and I had then to copy and translate the tablets as far as their mutilated condition would allow.

The Genesis legends which I had collected from the various Assyrian fragments included numerous other stories beside those which parallel the account in the Book of Genesis. All these stories are similar in character, and appear to belong to the same early literary age. So far as I have made out they are as follows:—

1. A long account of the origin of the world, the creation of the animals and man, the fall of man from a sinless state, and a conflict between the gods and the powers of evil.

2. A second account of the creation having a closer correspondence with the account of Berosus.

3. A Bilingual legend of the history of the seven evil spirits, apparently part of a third version of the creation.

4. Story of the descent of the goddess Ishtar or Venus into Hades, and her return.

5. Legend of the sin of the God Zu, who insults Elu, the father of the gods.

6. Collection of five tablets giving the exploits of Lubara the god of the pestilence.

7. Legend of the god Sarturda, who turned into a bird.

8. Story of the wise man who put forth a riddle to the gods.

9. Legend of the good man Atarpi, and the wickedness of the world.

10. Legend of the tower of Babel, and dispersion.

11. Story of the Eagle and Etana.

12. Story of the ox and the horse.

13. Story of the fox.

14. Legend of Sinuri.

15. Izdubar legends: twelve tablets, with the history of Izdubar, and an account of the flood.

16. Various fragments of other legends. These show that there was a considerable collection of such primitive stories almost unrepresented in our present collection.

CHAPTER II: BABYLONIAN AND ASSYRIAN LITERATURE.

Babylonian literature.—Kouyunjik library.—Fragmentary condition.—Arrangement of tablets.—Subjects.—Dates.—Babylonian source of literature.—Literary period.—Babylonian Chronology.—Akkad.—Sumir.—Urukh, king of Ur.—Hammurabi.—Babylonian astrology.—War of Gods.—Izdubar legends.—Creation and fall.—Syllabaries and bilingual tablets.—Assyrian copies.—Difficulties as to date.—Mutilated condition.—Babylonian library.—Assyrian empire.—City of Assur.—Library at Calah.—Sargon of Assyria.—Sennacherib.—Removal of Library to Nineveh.—Assurbanipal or Sardanapalus.—His additions to library.—Description of contents.—Later Babylonian libraries.

IN order to understand the position of these legends it is necessary to give some account of the wonderful literature of the Ancient Babylonians and their copyists, the Assyrians. The fragments of terra cotta tablets containing these legends were found in the débris which covers the palaces called the South West Palace and the North Palace at Kouyunjik; the former building being of the age of Sennacherib, the latter belonging to the time of Assurbanipal. The tablets, which are of all sizes, from one inch long to over a foot square, are nearly all in fragments, and in consequence of the changes which have taken place in the ruins the fragments of the same tablet are sometimes scattered widely apart. It appears from a consideration of the present positions of the fragments that they were originally in the upper chambers of the palace, and have fallen on the destruction of the building. In some of the lower chambers they lay covering the whole floor, in other cases they lay in groups or patches on the pavement, and there are occasional clusters of fragments at various heights in the earth which covers the buildings. The other fragments are scattered singly through all the upper earth which covers the floors and walls of the palace. Different fragments of the same tablets and cylinders are found in separate chambers which have no immediate connection with each other, showing that the present distribution of the fragments has nothing to do with the original position of the tablets.

A consideration of the inscriptions shows that these tablets have been arranged according to their subjects in various positions in the libraries. Stories or subjects were commenced on tablets and continued on other tablets of the same size and form, in some cases the number of tablets in a series and on a single subject amounting to over one hundred.

Each subject or series of tablets had a title, the title being formed by the first phrase or part of phrase in the subject. Thus, the series of Astrological tablets, numbering over seventy tablets, bore the title "When the gods Anu, Elu," this being the commencement of the first tablet. At the end of every tablet in each series was written its number in the work, thus: "the first tablet of "When the gods Anu, Elu," the second tablet of "When the gods Anu, Elu," &c. &c.; and, further to preserve the proper position of each tablet, every one except the last in a series had at the end a catch phrase, consisting of the first line of the following tablet. There were beside, catalogues of these documents written like them on clay tablets, and other small oval tablets with titles upon them, apparently labels for the various series of works. All these arrangements show the care taken with respect to literary matters. There were regular libraries or chambers, probably on the upper floors of the palaces, appointed for the store of the tablets, and custodians or librarians to take charge of them. It is probable that all these regulations were of great antiquity, and were copied like the tablets from the Babylonians.

Judging from the fragments discovered, it appears probable that there were in the Royal Library at Nineveh over 10,000 inscribed tablets, including almost every subject in ancient literature.

In considering a subject like the present one it is a point of the utmost importance to define as closely as possible the date of our present copies of the legends, and the most probable period at which the original copies may have been inscribed. By far the greatest number of the tablets brought from Nineveh belong to the age of Assurbanipal, who reigned over Assyria B.C. 670, and every copy of the Genesis legends yet found was inscribed during his reign. The statements on the present tablets are conclusive on this point, and have not been called in question, but it is equally stated and acknowledged on all hands that these tablets are not the originals, but are only copies from earlier texts. It is unfortunate that the date of the original copies is never preserved, and thus a wide door is thrown open for difference of opinion on this point. The Assyrians acknowledge themselves that this literature was borrowed from Babylonian sources, and of course it is to Babylonia we have to look to ascertain the approximate dates of the original documents. The difficulty here is increased by the following considerations: it appears that at an early period in Babylonian history a great literary development took place, and numerous works were produced which embodied the prevailing myths, religion, and science of that day. Written many of them in a noble style of poetry, and appealing to the strongest feelings of the people on one side, or registering the highest efforts of their science on the other, these texts became the standards for Babylonian literature, and later generations were content to copy these writings instead of making new works for themselves. Clay, the material on which they were written, was everywhere abundant, copies were multiplied, and by the veneration in which they were held these texts fixed and stereotyped the style of Babylonian literature, and the language in which they were written remained the classical style in the country down to the Persian conquest. Thus it happens that texts of Rim-agu, Sargon, and Hammurabi, who were one thousand years before Nebuchadnezzar and Nabonidus, show the same language as the texts of these later kings, there being no sensible difference in style to match the long interval between them.

There is, however, reason to believe that, although the language of devotion and literature remained fixed, the speech of the bulk of the people was gradually modified; and in the time of Assurbanipal, when the Assyrians copied the Genesis legends, the common speech of the day was in very different style. The private letters and despatches of this age which have been discovered differ widely from the language of the contemporary public documents and religious writings, showing the change the language had undergone since the style of these was fixed. We have a slightly similar case in England, where the language of devotion and the style of the Bible differ in several respects from those of the English of to-day.

These considerations show the difficulty of fixing the age of a document from its style, and the difficulty is further increased by the uncertainty which hangs over all Babylonian chronology.

Chronology is always a thorny subject, and dry and unsatisfactory to most persons beside; some notice must, however, be taken of it here, in order to show the reasons for the dates and epochs fixed upon for the Genesis legends.

In this case the later chronology is not in question, and it is best to start with the generally received date of about B.C. 1300 for the conquest of

Babylonia by Tugultininip, king of Assyria. Before this date we have a period of about 250 years, during which a foreign race ruled at Babylon. Berosus calls these foreigners Arabs, but nothing is known as to their original home or race. It is supposed that this race came into Babylonia, or obtained dominion there under a king named Hammurabi, whose date is thus fixed about B.C. 1550. Many scholars do not agree to this, and consider Hammurabi much more ancient; no one, however, fixes him later than the sixteenth century B.C., so that the date B.C. 1550 may be accepted as the most moderate one possible for the epoch of Hammurabi. The date of Hammurabi is of consequence in the question, because there is no evidence of these legends being written after his epoch.

This circumstance may be accounted for by the fact that during the period following the conquest of Hammurabi the government was in the hands of foreigners, and was much more centralized than it had been before, Babylon being, so far as we know, the sole capital, the great cities which had been centres of literature suffering a decline.

Before the time of Hammurabi, there ruled several races of kings, of whom we possess numerous monuments. These monarchs principally reigned at the cities of Ur, Karrak, Larsa, and Akkad. Their inscriptions do not determine the length of their rule, but they probably covered the period from B.C. 2000 to 1550. The name of the monarch in whose time we have the first satisfactory evidence of contemporary monuments is read Urukh, and in the present state of our researches he may be fixed B.C. 2000. It must, however, be remarked that many scholars place him at a much earlier date. From the time of Urukh to that of Hammurabi the title of honour principally taken by the kings is "King of Sumir and Akkad," that is, King of Lower and Upper Babylonia. It appears probable that previous to the reign of Urukh the two divisions of Sumir and Akkad were separate monarchies; and it is therefore likely that any literature written before B.C. 2000 will show evidences of this division.

The rough outlines of Babylonian chronology at this period may be arranged as follows, always bearing in mind that the different dates are the lowest we can fairly assume, and that several of them may be much more ancient:—

Down to B.C. 2000 epoch of independent kingdoms in Babylonia; the principal centre of activity being Akkad, a region on the Euphrates, somewhere between latitudes 32° and 33°.

B.C. 2000. Era of Urukh, king of Ur, rise of Sumir, the southern part of the country, Ur the metropolis.

B.C. 1850. Era of Ismi-dagan, king of Karrak, Karrak the metropolis.

B.C. 1700. Rise of Larsa as metropolis.

B.C. 1600. Era of Sargon, king of Akkad; revival of the power of Akkad.

B.C. 1550. Era of Hammurabi, king of Babylon. Babylon the metropolis.

Although we cannot fix the dates of any monuments before the time of Urukh, B.C. 2000, it is quite certain that there were buildings and inscriptions before that date; and there are two literary works which I should judge to be certainly older than this epoch, namely, the great Chaldean work on Astrology, and a legend which, for want of a better title, I call the Exploits of Lubara.

The Chaldean work, containing the bulk of their astrology, appears to belong to the northern half of the country, that is to Akkad, and always speaks of Akkad as a separate state, and implies it to be the leading state. It mentions besides, the kingdoms of Subartu, Martu, or Syria, Gutim or Goim, and Elam, and some parts, perhaps of later date than the body of the work, give also the kingdoms of Kassi, Kissati, or the peoples, Nituk or Asmun, Sumir, Yamutbal, and Assan. In the body of the work there appear glosses, apparently later additions, mentioning kings of the period B.C. 2000 to 1850. I have not noticed any gloss containing a royal name later than the kings of Ur.

The work I have provisionally called "The Exploits of Lubara," and which also bears evidence of great antiquity, is a much shorter one, for while there are over seventy large tablets of the astrology, this, on the other hand, only contained five small tablets. This work notices a large number of peoples or states, the principal being the people of the coast, Subartu, Assyria, Elam, Kassi, Sutu, Goim, Lullubu, Akkad; the uniting of Sumir and Akkad, which was accomplished at least B.C. 2000, is not mentioned, but the notice of the Assyrians is rather an argument for a later date than I have chosen.

The Izdubar legends, containing the story of the Flood, and what I believe to be the history of Nimrod, were probably written in the south of the country, and at least as early as B.C. 2000. These legends were, however, traditions before they were committed to writing, and were common in some form to all the country. The story of the Creation and Fall belongs to the upper or Akkad division of the country, and may not have been committed to writing so early as the Izdubar legends; but even this is of great antiquity.

About the same time as the account of the Creation, a series of tablets on evil spirits, which contained a totally different tradition of the Creation, was probably written; and there is a third account from the City of Cutha, closely agreeing in some respects with the account handed down by Berosus, which I should provisionally place about the same date. It seems, from the indications in the inscriptions, that there happened in the interval B.C. 2000 to 1850 a general collecting and development of the various traditions of the Creation, Flood, Tower of Babel, and other similar legends.

A little later, about B.C. 1600, a new set of astrological tablets was written, together with a long work on terrestrial omens; these appear to belong to the kingdom and period of Sargon, king of Akkad.

Some at least, and probably most of the syllabaries, bilingual and explanatory tablets, grammars and vocabularies, belong to this period also; but a few are of later date.

In spite of the indications as to peculiarities of worship, names of states and capitals, historical allusions and other evidence, it may seem hazardous to many persons to fix the dates of original documents so high, when our only copies in many cases are Assyrian transcripts made in the reign of Assurbanipal, in the seventh century B.C.; but one or two considerations may show that this is a perfectly reasonable view, and no other likely period can be found for the original composition of the documents unless we ascend to a greater antiquity. In the first place, it must be noticed that the Assyrians themselves state that the documents were copied from ancient Babylonian copies, and in some cases state that the old copies were partly illegible even in their day. Again, in one case there is actual proof of the antiquity of a text, an Assyrian copy of part of which is published in "Cuneiform Inscriptions," vol. ii. plate 54, Nos. 3 & 4. In a collection of tablets discovered by Mr. Loftus at Senkereh, belonging, according to the kings mentioned in it, to about B.C. 1600, is part of an ancient Babylonian copy of this very text, the Babylonian copy being about one thousand years older than the Assyrian one.

It is, however, probable that most of the legends treated of in the present volume had existed as traditions in the country long before they were committed to writing, and some of these traditions, as embodied in the various works, exhibit great difference in details, showing that they had passed through many changes.

Taking the period of literary development in Babylonia as extending from B.C. 2000 to 1550, we may say, it roughly synchronizes with the period from Abraham to Moses, according to the ordinary chronology of our Bibles, and during this period it appears that traditions of the creation of the universe, and human history down to the time of Nimrod, existed parallel to, and in some points identical with, those given in the Book of Genesis.

Many of the documents embodying these traditions have been discovered in sadly mutilated condition, but there can be no doubt that future explorations will reveal more perfect copies, and numerous companion and explanatory texts, which will one day clear up the difficulties which now meet us at every step of their consideration.

So far as known contemporary inscriptions are concerned, we cannot consider our present researches and discoveries as anything like sufficient to give a fair view of the literature of Assyria and Babylonia, and, however numerous and important are the Genesis legends, they form but a small portion of the whole literature of the country.

It is generally considered that the earliest inscriptions of any importance which we now possess belong to the time of Urukh, king of Ur, whose age may be placed with great probability about two thousand years before the Christian era.

The principal inscriptions of this period consist of texts on bricks and on signet cylinders, and some of the latter may be of much greater antiquity. Passing down to the period of the kingdoms of Karrak, Larsa, and Akkad, we find a great accession of literary material, almost every class of writing being represented by contemporary specimens. It is certain that even then the inscribed clay tablets were not isolated, but already they were arranged in collections or libraries, and these collections were placed at some of the principal cities. From Senkerch and its neighbourhood have come our earliest specimens of these literary tablets, the following being some of the contents of this earliest known library:—

1. Mythological tablets, including lists of the gods, and their manifestations and titles.

2. Grammatical works, lists of words, and explanations.

3. Mathematical works, calculations, tables, cube and square root, measures.

4. Astronomy, astrology, and omens.

5. Legends and short historical inscriptions.

6. Historical cylinders, one of Kudur-mabuk, B.C. 1600 (the earliest known cylinder), being in the British Museum.

7. Geographical tablets, and lists of towns and countries.

8. Laws and law cases, sale and barter, wills and loans.

Such are the inscriptions from the libraries of the early inhabitants of Babylonia, and beside these there are numerous texts, only known to us through later copies, but which certainly had their origin as early as this period.

Passing down from this period, for some centuries we find only detached inscriptions, accompanied by evidence of the gradual shifting both of the political power and literary activity from Babylonia to Assyria.

In Assyria the first centre of Literature and seat of a library was the city of Assur (Kileh Shergat), and the earliest known tablets date about B.C. 1500.

Beyond the scanty records of some of the monarchs nothing of value remains of this library for several centuries, and the Assyrian literary works are only known from later copies.

A revival of the Assyrian empire began under Assur-nazir-pal, king of Assyria, who ascended the throne B.C. 885. He rebuilt the city of Calah (Nimroud), and this city became the seat of an Assyrian library. Tablets were procured from Babylonia by Shalmaneser, son of Assur-nazir-pal, B.C. 860, during the reign of Nabu-bal-idina, king of Babylon, and these were copied by the Assyrian scribes, and placed in the royal library. Vul-nirari, grandson of Shalmaneser, B.C. 812, added to the Calah library, and had tablets written at Nineveh. Assurnirari, B.C. 755, continued the literary work, some mythological tablets being dated in his reign.

Tiglath Pileser, B.C. 745, enlarged the library, and placed in it various copies of historical inscriptions. It was, however, reserved for Sargon, who founded the last Assyrian dynasty, B.C. 722, to make the Assyrian royal library worthy of the empire. Early in his reign he appointed Nabu-suqub-gina principal librarian, and this officer set to work making new copies of all the standard works of the day. During the whole of his term of office copies of the great literary works were produced, the majority of the texts preserved belonging to the early period previous to B.C. 1600.

In the period which followed there was a general revival of all the ancient works which had escaped destruction, and the study of this early literature became a marked feature of the time.

Sennacherib, son of Sargon, B.C. 705, continued to add to his father's library at Calah, but late in his reign he removed the collection from that city to Nineveh, where from this time the national library remained until the fall of the empire.

Esarhaddon, son of Sennacherib, B.C. 681, further increased the national collection, most of his works being of a religious character.

Assurbanipal, son of Esarhaddon, the Sardanapalus of the Greeks, B.C. 673, was the greatest of the Assyrian sovereigns, and he is far more memorable on account of his magnificent patronage of learning than on account of the greatness of his empire or the extent of his wars.

Assurbanipal added more to the Assyrian royal library than all the kings who had gone before him, and it is to tablets written in his reign that we owe almost all our knowledge of the Babylonian myths and early history, beside many other important matters.

The agents of Assurbanipal sought everywhere for inscribed tablets, brought them to Nineveh, and copied them there; thus the literary treasures of Babylon, Borsippa, Cutha, Akkad, Ur, Erech, Larsa, Nipur and various other cities were transferred to the Assyrian capital to enrich the great collection there.

The fragments brought over to Europe give us a good idea of this library and show the range of the subjects embraced by this collection of inscriptions. Among the different classes of texts, the Genesis stories and similar legends occupied a prominent place; these, as they will be further described in the present volume, need only be mentioned here. Accompanying them we have a series of mythological tablets of various sorts, varying from legends of the gods, psalms, songs, prayers, and hymns, down to mere allusions and lists of names. Many of these texts take the form of charms to be used in sickness and for the expulsion of evil spirits; some of them are of great antiquity, being at least as old as the creation and Izdubar legends. One fine series concerns the cure of witchcraft, a superstition fully believed in in those days. Izdubar is mentioned in one of these tablets as lord of the oaths or pledges of the world.

Some of the prayers were for use on special occasions, such as on starting on a campaign, on the occurrence of an eclipse, &c. Astronomy and Astrology were represented by various detached inscriptions and reports, but principally by the great work on these subjects covering over seventy tablets which was borrowed from the early Chaldeans, and many copies of which were in the Library of Assurbanipal. This work on Astrology and Astronomy was, as I have already stated, one of the most ancient texts in the Euphrates valley.

There were also numerous copies of a long work on Terrestrial omens, which appears to date from the time of Sargon, king of Akkad, about B.C. 1600. In this work everything in nature is supposed to portend some coming event.

There is a fragment of one Astrological tablet which professes to be copied from an original of the time of Izdubar.

Historical texts formed another section of the library, and these included numerous copies of inscriptions of early Babylonian kings; there were beside, chronological tablets with lists of kings and annual officers, inscriptions of various Assyrian monarchs, histories of the relations between Assyria and Babylonia, Elam, and Arabia, treaties, despatches, proclamations. and reports on the state of the empire and military affairs.

Natural history was represented by tables of animals; mammals, birds, reptiles, fishes, insects, and plants, trees, grasses, reeds, and grains, earths, stones, &c. These lists are classified according to the supposed nature and affinities of the various species, and show considerable advance in the sciences. Mathematics had a place in the library, there being problems, figures, and calculations; but this branch of learning was not studied so fully as in Babylonia.

Grammar and Lexicography were better represented, there being many works do these subjects, including lists of the signs and explanations, declension of nouns, conjugation of verbs, examples of syntax, bilingual tables, explanatory lists, &c. All these tablets were copied from the Babylonians. In law and civil matters the library was also rich, and the tablets serve to show that the same laws and customs prevailed in Assyria as in Babylonia. There are codes of laws law cases, sale, barter, loans, lists of property, lists of titles and trades, tribute, and taxes, &c.

In Geography the Assyrians were not very forward; but there are lists of countries and their productions, of cities, rivers, mountains, and peoples.

Such are some of the principal contents of the great library from which we have obtained our copies of the Creation and Flood legends, most of the tablets were copied from early Babylonian inscriptions, the original copies of the works have in most cases disappeared; but these remarkable inscriptions have preserved to us texts which show the wonderful advance made by the people of Chaldea before the time of Moses. Babylonian literature, which had been the parent of Assyrian writing, revived after the fall of Nineveh, and Nebuchadnezzar and his successors 'made Babylon the seat of a library rivalling that of Assurbanipal at Nineveh. Of this later development of Babylonian literature we know very little, explorations being still required to bring to light the texts of this epoch. Few fragments only, discovered by wandering Arabs or recovered by chance travellers, have yet turned up, but there is in them evidence enough to promise a rich reward to future excavators.

CHAPTER III: CHALDEAN LEGENDS TRANSMITTED THROUGH BEROSUS AND OTHER ANCIENT AUTHORS.

Berosus and his copyists.—Cory's translation.—Alexander Polyhistor.—Babylonia.—Oannes, his teaching.—Creation.—Belus.— Chaldean kings.—Xisuthrus.—Deluge.—The Ark.—Return to Babylon.—Apollodorus.—Pantibiblon.—Larancha.—Abydenus.— Alorus, first king.—Ten kings.—Sisithrus.—Deluge.—Armenia.— Tower of Babel.—Cronos and Titan.—Nicolaus Damascenes.— Dispersion from Hestiæus.—Babylonian colonies.—Tower of Babel.— The Sibyl.—Titan and Prometheus.—Damascius.—Tauthe.— Moymis.—Kissare and Assorus.—Triad.—Bel.

I HAVE included in this chapter the principal extracts from ancient authors respecting the Babylonian accounts of Genesis. Many others are known, but are of doubtful origin, and of less immediate interest to my subject.

Berosus, from whom the principal extracts are copied, lived, as I have mentioned in Chapter I., about B.C. 330 to 260, and, from his position as a Babylonian priest, had the best means of knowing the Babylonian traditions.

The others are later writers, who copied in the main from Berosus, and whose notices may be taken as giving abridgments of his statements.

I have preferred as usual, the translations of Cory as being standard ones, and made without prejudice from recent discoveries.

EXTRACT I. FROM ALEXANDER POLYHISTOR (CORY, p. 21).

Berosus, in the first book of his history of Babylonia, informs us that he lived in the age of Alexander, the son of Philip. And he mentions that there were written accounts, preserved at Babylon with the greatest care, comprehending a period of above fifteen myriads of years; and that these writings contained histories of the heaven and of the sea; of the birth of mankind; and of the kings, and of the memorable actions which they had achieved.

And in the first place he describes Babylonia as a country situated between the Tigris and the Euphrates; that it abounded with wheat, and barley, and ocrus, and sesame; and that in the lakes were produced the roots called gongæ, which are fit for food, and in respect to nutriment similar to barley. That there were also palm-trees and apples, and a variety of fruits; fish also and birds, both those which are merely of flight, and those which frequent the lakes. He adds that those parts of the country which bordered upon Arabia were without water, and barren; but that the parts which lay on the other side were both hilly and fertile.

At Babylon there was (in these times) a great resort of people of various nations, who inhabited Chaldea, and lived in a lawless manner like the beasts of the field.

In the first year there appeared, from that part of the Erythræan sea which borders upon Babylonia, an animal endowed with reason, by name Oannes, whose whole body (according to the account of Apollodorus) was that of a fish; that under the fish's head he had another head, with feet also below similar to those of a man, subjoined to the fish's tail. His voice, too, and language were articulate and human; and a representation of him is preserved even to this day.

This being was accustomed to pass the day among men, but took no food at that season; and he gave them an insight into letters and sciences, and arts of every kind. He taught them to construct cities, to found temples, to compile laws, and explained to them the principles of geometrical knowledge. He made them distinguish the seeds of the earth, and showed them how to collect the fruits; in short, he instructed them in every thing which could tend to soften manners and humanize their lives. From that time, nothing material has been added by way of improvement to his instructions. And when the sun had set this being Oannes retired again into the sea, and passed the night in the deep, for he was amphibious. After this there appeared other animals like Oannes, of which Berosus proposes to give an account when he comes to the history of the kings. Moreover, Oannes wrote concerning the generation of mankind, and of their civil polity; and the following is the purport of what he said:—

"There was a time in which there existed nothing but darkness and an abyss of waters, wherein resided most hideous beings, which were produced of a two-fold principle. There appeared men, some of whom were furnished with two wings, others with four, and with two faces. They had one body, but two heads; the one that of a man, the other of a woman; and likewise in their several organs both male and female. Other human figures were to be seen with the legs and horns of a goat; some had horses' feet, while others united the hind quarters of a horse with the body of a man, resembling in shape the hippocentaurs. Bulls likewise were bred there with the heads of men; and dogs with fourfold bodies, terminated in their extremities with the tails of fishes; horses also with the heads of dogs; men, too, and other animals, with the heads and bodies of horses, and the tails of fishes. In short, there were creatures in which were combined the limbs of every species of animals. In addition to these, fishes, reptiles, serpents, with other monstrous animals, which assumed each other's shape and countenance. Of all which were preserved delineations in the temple of Belus at Babylon.

"The person who presided over them was a woman named Omoroca, which in the Chaldean language is Thalatth, in Greek Thalassa, the sea; but which might equally be interpreted the moon. All things being in this situation, Belus came, and cut the woman asunder, and of one half of her he formed the earth, and of the other half the heavens, and at the same time destroyed the animals within her (or in the abyss).

"All this" (he says) "was an allegorical description of nature. For, the whole universe consisting of moisture, and animals being continually generated therein, the deity above-mentioned took off his own head; upon which the other gods mixed the blood, as it gushed out, and from thence formed men. On this account it is that they are rational, and partake of divine knowledge. This Belus, by whom they signify Jupiter, divided the darkness, and separated the heavens from the earth, and reduced the universe to order. But the animals, not being able to bear the prevalence of light, died. Belus upon this, seeing a vast space unoccupied, though by nature fruitful, commanded one of the gods to take off his head, and to mix the blood with the earth, and from thence to form other men and animals, which should be capable of bearing the air. Belus formed also the stars, and the sun, and the moon, and the five planets." (Such, according to Polyhistor Alexander, is the account which Berosus gives in his first book.)

(In the second book was contained the history of the ten kings of the Chaldeans, and the periods of the continuance of each reign, which consisted collectively of an hundred and twenty sari, or four hundred and thirty-two thousand years; reaching to the time of the Deluge. For Alexander, enumerating the kings from the writings of the Chaldeans, after the ninth Ardates, proceeds to the tenth, who is called by them Xisuthrus, in this manner):—

"After the death of Ardates, his son Xisuthrus . reigned eighteen sari. In his time happened a great deluge; the history of which is thus described.

The deity Cronos appeared to him in a vision, and warned him that upon the fifteenth day of the month Dæsius there would be a flood, by which mankind would be destroyed. He therefore enjoined him to write a history of the beginning, procedure, and conclusion of all things, and to bury it in the city of the Sun at Sippara; and to build a vessel, and take with him into it his friends and relations; and to convey on board every thing necessary to sustain life, together with all the different animals, both birds and quadrupeds, and trust himself fearlessly to the deep. Having asked the Deity whither he was to sail, he was answered, 'To the Gods;' upon which he offered up a prayer for the good of mankind. He then obeyed the divine admonition, and built a vessel five stadia in length, and two in breadth. Into this he put everything which he had prepared, and last of all conveyed into it his wife, his children, and his friends.

After the flood had been upon the earth, and was in time abated, Xisuthrus sent out birds from the vessel; which not finding any food, nor any place whereupon they might rest their feet, returned to him again. After an interval of some days, he sent them forth a second time; and they now returned with their feet tinged with mud. He made a trial a third time with these birds; but they returned to him no more: from whence he judged that the surface of the earth had appeared above the waters. He therefore made an opening in the vessel, and upon looking out found that it was stranded upon the side of some mountain; upon which he immediately quitted it with his wife, his daughter, and the pilot. Xisuthrus then paid his adoration to the earth: and, having constructed an altar, offered sacrifices to the gods, and, with those who had come out of the vessel with him, disappeared.

They, who remained within, finding that their companions did not return, quitted the vessel with many lamentations, and called continually on the name of Xisuthrus. Him they saw no more; but they could distinguish his voice in the air, and could hear him admonish them to pay due regard to religion; and likewise informed them that it was upon account of his piety that he was translated to live with the gods, that his wife and daughter and the pilot had obtained the same honour. To this he added that they should return to Babylonia, and, as it was ordained, search for the writings at Sippara, which they were to make known to all mankind; moreover, that the place wherein they then were was the land of Armenia. The rest having heard these words offered sacrifices to the gods, and, taking a circuit, journeyed towards Babylonia.

The vessel being thus stranded in Armenia, some part of it yet remains in the Corcyræan mountains of Armenia, and the people scrape off the bitumen with which it had been outwardly coated, and make use of it by way of an alexipharmic and amulet. And when they returned to Babylon and had found the writings at Sippara they built cities and erected temples, and Babylon was thus inhabited again.—*Syncel. Chron.* xxviii.; *Euseb. Chron.* v. 8.

BEROSUS, FROM APOLLODORUS (CORY, p. 30).

This is the history which Berosus has transmitted to us. He tells us that the first king was Alorus of Babylon, a Chaldean, he reigned ten sari; and afterwards Alaparus and Amelon, who came from Pantebiblon; then Ammenon the Chaldean, in whose time appeared the Musarus Oannes, the Annedotus from the Erythræan sea. (But Alexander Polyhistor, anticipating the event, has said that he appeared in the first year, but Apollodorus says that it was after forty sari; Abydenus, however, makes the second Annedotus appear after twenty-six sari.) Then succeeded Megalarus from the city of Pantibiblon, and he reigned eighteen sari; and after him Daonus, the shepherd from Pantibiblon, reigned ten sari; in his time (he says) appeared again from the Erythræan sea a fourth Annedotus, having the same form with those above, the shape of a fish blended with that of a man. Then reigned Euedorachus from Pantibiblon for the term of eighteen sari; in his days there appeared another personage from the Erythræan sea like the former, having the same complicated form between a fish and a man, whose name was Odacon. (All these, says Apollodorus, related particularly and circumstantially whatever Oannes had informed them of; concerning these Abydenus has made no mention.) Then reigned Amempsinus, a Chaldean from Larancha; and he being the eighth in order reigned ten sari. Then reigned Otiartes, a Chaldean, from Larancha; and he reigned eight sari. And, upon the death of Otiartes, his son Xisuthrus reigned eighteen sari; in his time happened the great Deluge. So that the sum of all the kings is ten; and the term which they collectively reigned an hundred and twenty sari.—*Syncel. Chron.* xxxix.; *Euseb. Chron.* V.

BEROSUS, FROM ABYDENUS (CORY, p. 32).

So much concerning the wisdom of the Chaldeans.

It is said that the first king of the country was Alorus, and that he gave out a report that God had appointed him to be the shepherd of the people, he reigned ten sari; now a sarus is esteemed to be three thousand six hundred years, a neros six hundred, and a sossus sixty.

After him Alaparus reigned three sari; to him succeeded Amillarus from the city of Pantibiblon, who reigned thirteen sari; in his time came up from the sea a second Annedotus, a semi-demon very similar in his form to Oannes; after Amillarus reigned Ammenon twelve sari, who was of the city of Pantibiblon; then Megalarus of the same place reigned eighteen sari; then Daos the shepherd governed for the space of ten sari, he was of Pantibiblon; in his time four double-shaped personages came up out of the sea to land, whose names were Euedocus, Eneugamus, Eneuboulus, and Anementus; afterwards in the time of Euedoreschus appeared another, Anodaphus. After these reigned other kings, and last of all Sisithrus, so that in the whole the number amounted to ten kings, and the term of their reigns to an hundred and twenty sari. (And among other things not irrelative to the subject he continues thus concerning the Deluge): After Euedoreschus some others reigned, and then Sisithrus. To him the deity Cronos foretold that on the fifteenth day of the month Dæsius there would be a deluge of rain: and he commanded him to deposit all the writings whatever which were in his possession in the city of the sun in Sippara. Sisithrus, when he had complied with these commands, sailed immediately to Armenia, and was presently inspired by God. Upon the third day after the cessation of the rain Sisithrus sent out birds by way of experiment, that he might judge whether the flood had subsided. But the birds, passing over an unbounded sea without finding any place of rest, returned again to Sisithrus. This he repeated with other birds. And when upon the third trial he succeeded, for the birds then returned with their feet stained with mud, the gods translated him from among men. With respect to the vessel, which yet remains in Armenia, it is a custom of the inhabitants to form bracelets and amulets of its wood.—*Syncel. Chron.* xxxviii.; *Euseb. Præp. Evan.* lib. ix.; *Euseb. Chron.* v. 8.

OF THE TOWER OF BABEL (CORY, p. 34).

They say that the first inhabitants of the earth, glorying in their own strength and size and despising the gods, undertook to raise a tower whose top should reach the sky, in the place in which Babylon now stands; but when it approached the heaven the winds assisted the gods, and overthrew the work upon its contrivers, and its ruins are said to be still at Babylon; and the gods introduced a diversity of tongues among men, who till that time had all spoken the same language; and a war arose between Cronos and Titan. The place in which they built the tower is now called Babylon on account of the confusion of tongues, for confusion is by the Hebrews called Babel.—*Euseb. Præp. Evan.* lib. ix.; *Syncel. Chron.* xliv.; *Euseb. Chron.* xiii.

OF THE ARK, FROM NICOLAUS DAMASCENUS (CORY, p. 49).

There is above Minyas in the land of Armenia a very great mountain which is called Baris, to which it is said that many persons retreated at the time of the Deluge and were saved, and that one in particular was carried thither in an ark and was landed on its summit, and that the remains of the vessel were long preserved upon the mountain. Perhaps this was the same individual of whom Moses, the legislator of the Jews, has made mention.—*Jos. Ant. Jud.* i. 3; *Euseb. Præp. Evan.* ix.

OF THE DISPERSION, FROM HESTIÆUS (CORY, p. 50).

The priests who escaped took with them the implements of the worship of the Enyalian Jove, and came to Senaar in Babylonia. But they were again driven from thence by the introduction of a diversity of tongues; upon which they founded colonies in various parts, each settling in such situations as chance or the direction of God led them to occupy.—*Jos. Ant. Jud. i.e.* 4; *Euseb. Præp. Evan.* ix,

OF THE TOWER OF BABEL, FROM ALEXANDER POLYHISTOR CORY, p. 50) .

The Sibyl says: That when all men formerly spoke the same language some among them undertook to erect a large and lofty tower, that they might climb up into heaven. But God sending forth a whirlwind confounded their design, and gave to each tribe a particular language of its own, which is the reason that the name of that city is Babylon. After the deluge lived Titan and Prometheus, when Titan undertook a war against Cronus.—*Sync.* xliv.; *Jos. Ant. Jud.* i. c. 4; *Euseb. Præp. Evan.* ix.

THE THEOGONIES, FROM DAMASCIUS (CORY, p. 318).

But the Babylonians, like the rest of the barbarians, pass over in silence the One principle of the universe, and they constitute two, Tauthe and Apason, making Apason the husband of Tauthe, and denominating her the mother of the gods. And from these proceeds an only-begotten son, Moymis, which I conceive is no other than the intelligible world proceeding from the two principles. From them also another progeny is derived, Dache and Dachus; and again a third, Kissare and Assorus, from which last three others proceed, Anus, and Illinus, and Aus. And of Aus and Davce is born a son called Belus, who, they say, is the fabricator of the world, the Demiurgus.

CHAPTER IV: BABYLONIAN MYTHOLOGY.

Greek accounts.—Mythology local in origin.—Antiquity.—
Conquests.—Colonies.—Three great gods.—Twelve great gods.—
Angels.—Spirits.—Anu.—Anatu.—Vul.—Ishtar.—Equivalent to
Venus.—Hea.—Oannes.—Merodach.—Bel or Jupiter.—Zirat-banit,
Succoth Benoth.—Elu.—Sin the moon god.—Ninip.—Shamas.—
Nergal.—Anunit.—Table of gods.

IN their accounts of the Creation and of the early history of the human race the Babylonian divinities figure very prominently, but it is difficult in many cases to identify the deities mentioned by the Greek authors, because the phonetic reading of the names of the Babylonian gods is very obscure, and the classical writers often mention these divinities by the terms in their own mythology, which appeared to them to correspond with the Babylonian names.

In this chapter it is only proposed to give a general account of some parts of the Babylonian mythology, to show the relationship between the deities and their titles and work.

Babylonian mythology was local in origin; each of the gods had a particular city which was the seat of his worship, and it is probable that the idea of weaving the gods into a system, in which each should have his part to play, only had its origin at a later time. The antiquity of this mythology may be seen by the fact, that two thousand years before the Christian era it was already completed, and its deities definitely connected into a system which remained with little change down to the close of the kingdom.

It is probable that the gods were in early times only worshipped at their original cities or seats, the various cities or settlements being independent of each other; but it was natural as wars arose, and some cities gained conquests over others, and kings gradually united the country into monarchies, that the people of conquering cities should claim that their gods were superior to those of the cities they conquered, and thus carne the system of different ranks or grades among the gods. Again, colonies were sent out of some cities, and the colonies, as they considered themselves sons of the cities they started from, also considered their gods to be sons of the gods of the mother cities. Political changes in early times led to the rise and fall of various cities and consequently of their deities, and gave rise to numerous myths relating to the different personages in the mythology. In some remote age there appear to have been three great cities in the country, Erech, Eridu, and Nipur, and their divinities Anu, Hea, and Bel were considered the "great gods" of the country. Subsequent changes led to the decline of these cities, but their deities still retained their position at the head of the Babylonian system.

These three leading deities formed members of a circle of twelve gods, also called great. These gods and their titles are given as:

1. Anu, king of angels and spirits, lord of the city of Erech.

2. Bel, lord of the world, father of the gods, creator, lord of the city of Nipur.

3. Hea, maker of fate, lord of the deep, god of wisdom and knowledge, lord of the city of Eridu.

4. Sin, lord of crowns, maker of brightness, lord of the city of Ur.

5. Merodach, just prince of the gods, lord of birth, lord of the city of Babylon.

6. Vul, the strong god, lord of canals and atmosphere, lord of the city of Muru.

7. Shamas, judge of heaven and earth, director of all, lord of the cities of Larsa and Sippara.

8. Ninip, warrior of the warriors of the gods, destroyer of wicked, lord of the city of Nipur.

9. Nergal, giant king of war, lord of the city of Cutha.

10. Nusku, holder of the golden sceptre, the lofty god.

11. Belat, wife of Bel, mother of the great gods, lady of the city of Nipur.

12. Ishtar, eldest of heaven and earth, raising the face of warriors.

Below these deities there was a large body of gods forming the bulk of the pantheon, and below these were arranged the Igege, or angels of heaven, and the Anunnaki, or angels of earth. Below these again came various classes of spirits or genii called Sedu, Vadukku, Ekimu, Gallu, and others; some of these were evil, some good.

The relationship of the various principal gods and their names, titles, and offices will be seen by the following remarks.

At the head of the Babylonian mythology stands a deity who was sometimes identified with the heavens, sometimes considered as the ruler and god of heaven. This deity is named Anu, his sign is the simple star, the symbol of divinity, and at other times the Maltese cross. Anu represents abstract divinity, and he appears as an original principle, perhaps as the original principle of nature. He represents the universe as the upper and lower regions, and when these were divided the upper region or heaven was called Anu, while the lower region or earth was called Anatu; Anatu being the female principle or wife of Anu. Anu is termed the old god, and the god of the whole of heaven and earth; one of the manifestations of Arm was as the two forms Lahma and Lahama, which probably correspond to the Greek forms Dache and Dachus. These forms are said to have sprung out of the original chaos, and they are followed by the two forms sar and kisar (the Kissare and Assorus of the Greeks), sar means the upper hosts or expanse, kisar the lower hosts or expanse; these are also forms of manifestations of Anu and his wife. Aim is also lord of the old city, and he bears the names Alalu and Papsukul. His titles generally indicate height, antiquity, purity, divinity, and he may be taken as the general type of divinity. Anu was originally worshipped at the city of Erech, which was called the city of Anu and Anatu, and the great temple there was called the "house of Anu," or the "house of heaven."

Anatu, the wife or consort of Anu, is generally only a female form of Anu, but is sometimes contrasted with him; thus, when Anu represents height and heaven, Anatu represents depth and earth; she is also lady of darkness, the mother of the god Hea, the mother producing heaven and earth, the female fish-god, and she is one of the many goddesses called Istar or Venus.

Anu and Anatu have a numerous family; among their sons are numbered Sar-ziri, the king of the desert, Latarak, Abgula, Kusu, and the air-god, whose name is uncertain. The air-god is usually called Vul, he has also the name Pur, and the epithets Ramman or Rimmon, the self-existent, and Uban or Ben. Vul is god of the region of the atmosphere, or space between the heaven and earth, he is the god of rain, of storms and whirlwind, of thunder and lightning, of floods and watercourses. Vul was in high esteem in Syria and Arabia, where he bore the name of Daddi; in Armenia he was called Teiseba. Vul is always considered an active deity, and was extensively worshipped.

Another important god, a son of Anu, was the god of fire; his name may be read Bil-kan, with the possibility of some connection with the Biblical Tubal Cain and the classical Vulcan. The fire-god takes an active part in the numerous mythological tablets and legends, and he is considered to be the most potent deity in relation to witchcraft and spells generally.

The most important of the daughters of Anu was named Istar; she was in some respects the equivalent of the classical Venus. Her worship was at first subordinate to that of Anu, and as she was goddess of love, while Anu was god of heaven, it is probable that the first intention in the mythology was only to represent love as heaven-born; but in time a more sensual view prevailed, and the worship of Istar became one of the darkest features in Babylonian mythology. As the worship of this goddess increased in favour, it gradually superseded that of Anu, until in time his temple, the house of heaven, came to be regarded as the temple of Venus.

The planet Venus, as the evening star, was identified with the Ishtar of Erech, while the morning star was Anunit, goddess of Akkad.

There were various other goddesses called Istar, among which may be noticed Istar, daughter of Sin the moon-god, who is sometimes confounded with the daughter of Anu.

A companion deity with Anu is Hea, who is god of the sea and of Hades, in fact of all the lower regions. He has two features, and corresponds in some respects to the Saturn or Cronos of the ancients, in others to their Poseidon or Neptune. Hea is called god of the lower region, he is lord of the sea or abyss; he is lord of generation and of all human beings, he bears the titles lord of wisdom, of mines and treasures; he is lord of gifts, of music, of fishermen and sailors, and of Hades or hell. It has been supposed that the serpent was one of his emblems, and that he was the Oannes of Berosus; these things do not, however, appear in the inscriptions. The wife of Hea was Dav-kina, the Davke of Damascius, who is the goddess of the lower regions, the consort of the deep; and their principal son was Maruduk or Merodach, the Bel of later times.

Merodach, god of Babylon, appears in all the earlier inscriptions as the agent of his father Hea; he goes about in the world collecting information, and receives commissions from his father to set right all that appears wrong. Merodach is an active agent in creation, but is always subordinate to his father Hea. In later times, after Babylon had been made the capital, Merodach, who was god of that city, was raised to the head of the Pantheon. Merodach or Bel was identified with the classical Jupiter, but the name Bel, "the lord," was only given to him in times subsequent to the rise of Babylon. The wife of Merodach was Zirat-banit, the Succoth Benoth of the Bible.

Nebo, the god of knowledge and literature, who was worshipped at the neighbouring city of Borsippa, was a favourite deity in later times, as was also his consort Tasmit. Beside Merodach Hea had a numerous progeny, his sons being principally river gods.

A third great god was united with Anu and Hea, his names were Enu, Elu, Kaptu, and Bel; he was the original Bel of the Babylonian mythology, and was lord of the surface of the earth and the affairs of men. Elu was lord of the city of Nipur, and had a consort named Belat or Beltis. Elu, or Bel, is the most active of the gods in the general affairs of mankind, and was so generally worshipped in early times that he came to be regarded as the national divinity, and his temple at the city of Nipur was regarded as the type of all temples. The extensive worship of Bel, and the high honour in which he was held, seem to point to a time when his city, Nipur, was the metropolis of the country.

Belat, or Beltis, the wife of Bel, is a famous deity celebrated in all ages, but as the title Belat was only "lady," or "goddess," it was a common one for many goddesses, and the notices of Beltis probably refer to several different personages. The same remark may be applied to the name Istar, or Ishtar, meaning "goddess," which is applied to any female divinity.

Elu had, like the other gods, a numerous family; his eldest son was the moon-god called Ur, Agu or Aku, Sin and Itu, in later times generally termed Sin. Sin was presiding deity of the city of Ur, and early assumed an important place in the mythology. The moon-god figures prominently in some early legends, and during the time the city of Ur was capital of the country his worship became very extensive and popular in the whole of the country.

Ninip, god of hunting and war, was another celebrated son of Elu; he was worshipped with his father at Nipur. Ninip was also much worshipped in Assyria as well as Babylonia, his character as presiding genius of war and the chase making him a favourite deity with the warlike kings of Assur.

Sin the moon-god had a son Shamas, or Samas, the sun-god, and a daughter, Istar or Venus. Shamas is an active deity in some of the Izdubar legends and fables, but he is generally subordinate to Sin. In the Babylonian system the moon takes precedence of the sun, and the Shamas of Larsa was probably considered a different deity to Shamas of Sippara.

Among the other deities of the Babylonians may be counted Nergal, god of Cutha, who, like Ninip, presided over hunting and war, and Anunit, the deity of one city of Sippara, and of the city of Akkad.

CHAPTER V: BABYLONIAN LEGEND OF THE CREATION.

Mutilated condition of tablets.—List of subjects.—Description of chaos.—Tiamat.—Generation of gods.—Damascius.—Comparison with Genesis.—Three great gods.—Doubtful fragments.—Fifth tablet.—Stars.—Planets.—Moon.—Sun.—Abyss or chaos.—Creation of moon,—Creation of animals.—Man.—His duties.—Dragon of sea.—Fall.—Curse for disobedience.—Discussion.—Sacred tree.— Dragon or serpent.—War with Tiamat.—Weapons.—Merodach.— Destruction of Tiamat.—Mutilation of documents.—Parallel Biblical account.—Age of story.

I HAVE related in the first chapter the history of the discovery of this legend; the tablets composing it are in mutilated condition, and too fragmentary to enable a single tablet to be completed, or to give more than a general view of the whole subject. The story, so far as I can judge from the fragment, agrees generally with the account of the Creation in the Book of Genesis, but shows traces of having originally included very much more matter. The fragments of the story which I have arranged are as follows:—

1. Part of the first tablet, giving an account of the Chaos and the generation of the gods.

2. Fragment of subsequent tablet, perhaps the second on the foundation of the deep.

3. Fragment of tablet placed here with great doubt, probably referring to the creation of land.

4. Part of the fifth tablet, giving the creation of the heavenly bodies.

5. Fragment of seventh? tablet, giving the creation of land animals.

6. Fragments of three tablets on the creation and fall of man.

7. Fragments of tablets relating to the war between the gods and evil spirits.

These fragments indicate that the series included at least twelve tablets, the writing on each tablet being in one column on the front and back, and probably including over one hundred lines of text.

The first fragment in the story is the upper part of the first tablet, giving the description of the void or chaos, and part of the generation of the gods. The translation is:

1. When above, were not raised the heavens:

2. and below on the earth a plant had not grown up;

3. the abyss also had not broken open their boundaries:

4. The chaos (or water) Tiamat (the sea) was the producing-mother of the whole of them.

5. Those waters at the beginning were ordained; but

6. a tree had not grown, a flower had not unfolded.

7. When the gods had not sprung up, any one of them;

8. a plant had not grown, and order did not exist;

9. Were made also the great gods,

10. the gods Lahmu and Lahamu they caused to come . . . . .

11. and they grew . . . . . .

12. the gods Sar and Kisar were made . . . .

13. A course of days, and a long time passed . . .

14. the god Anu . . . . . .

15. the gods Sar and . . . . . .

16. . . . . . .

On the reverse of this tablet there are only fragments of the eight lines of colophon, but the restoration of the passage is easy, it reads:—

1. First tablet of "When above" (name of Creation series).

2. Palace of Assurbanipal king of nations, king of Assyria,

3. to whom Nebo and Tasmit attentive ears have given:

4. he sought with diligent eyes the wisdom of the inscribed tablets,

5. which among the kings who went before me,

6. none those writings had sought.

7. The wisdom of Nebo, the impressions? of the god my instructor? all delightful,

8. on tablets I wrote, I studied, I observed, and

9. for the inspection of my people within my palace I placed

This colophon will serve to show the value attached to the documents, and the date of the present copies. The fragment of the obverse, broken as it is, is precious as giving the description of the chaos or desolate void before the Creation of the world, and the first movement of creation. This corresponds to the first two verses of the first chapter of Genesis.

1. "In the beginning God created the heaven and the earth.

2. And the earth was without form and void; and darkness was upon the face of the deep. And the spirit of God moved upon the face of the waters."

On comparing the fragment of the first tablet of the Creation with the extract front Damascius, we do not find any statement as to there being two principles at first called Tauthe and Apason, and these producing Moymis, but in the Creation tablet the first existence is called Mummu Tiamatu, a name meaning the "sea-water" or "sea chaos." The name Mummu Tiamatu combines the two names Moymis and Tauthe of Damascius. Tiamatu appears also as Tisallat and agrees with the Thalatth of Berosus, which we are expressly told was the sea. It is evident that, according to the notion of the Babylonians, the sea was the origin of all things, and this also agrees with the statement of Genesis, i. 2. where the chaotic waters are called תהום, "the deep," the same word as the Tiamat of the Creation text and the Tauthe of Damascius.

The Assyrian word *Mummu* is probably connected with the Hebrew המוהם, confusion, and one of its equivalents is *Umun*, equal to the Hebrew ורמה noise or tumult. Beside the name of the chaotic deep called והת in Genesis, which is, as I have said, evidently the Tiamat of the Creation text, we have in Genesis the word והב, waste, desolate, or formless, applied to this chaos. This appears to be the tehuta of the Assyrians—a name of the sea-water ("History of Assurbanipal," p. 59); this word is closely connected with the word tiamat or tamtu, the sea. The correspondence between the inscription and Genesis is here complete, both stating that a watery chaos preceded the creation, and formed, in fact, the origin and groundwork of the universe. We have here not only an agreement in sense, but, what is rarer, the same word used in both narratives as the name of this chaos, and given also in the account of Damascius. Berosus has certainly the slightly different form Thalatth, with the same sense however, and it might be suspected that this word was a corruption of Tiamat, but the Babylonian word is read Tiamtu, Tiamat, and Tisallat, which last is more probably the origin of the word Thalatth of Berosus.

Next we have in the inscription the creation of the gods Lahma or Lahmu, and Lahama or Lahamu; these are male and female personifications of motion and production, and correspond to the Dache and Dachus of Damascius, and the moving חור, wind, or spirit of Genesis. The next stage in the inscription gives the production of Sar or Ilsar, and Kisar, representing the upper expanse and the lower expanse, and corresponding to the Assorus and Kissare of Damascius. The resemblance in these names is probably closer than here represented, for Sar or Ilsar is generally read Assur as a deity in later times, being an ordinary sign for the supreme god of the Assyrians.

Here the cuneiform text becomes so mutilated that little can be made out from it, but it appears from the fragment of line 14 that the next step was (as in Damascius) the generation of the three great gods, Anu, Elu, and Hea, the Anus, Illinus, and Aus of that writer. Anu represents the heaven, Elu the earth, and Hea the sea, in this new form of the universe.

It is probable that the inscription went on to relate the generation of the other gods, and then passed to the successive acts of creation by which the world was fashioned.

The successive forms Lahma and Lahama, Sar and Kisar, are represented in some of the god lists as names or manifestations of Anu and Anatu. In each case there appears to be a male and female principle, which principles combine in the formation of the universe.

The resemblance between the extract from Damascius and the account in the Creation tablet as to these successive stages or forms in the Creation, is striking, and leaves no doubt that there was a connection between the two.

The three next tablets in the Creation series are absent, there being only two doubtful fragments of this part of the story. Judging from the analogy of the Book of Genesis, we may conjecture that this part of the narrative contained the description of the creation of light, of the atmosphere or firmament, of the dry land, and of plants. One fragment to which I have alluded as probably belonging to this space is a small portion of the top of a tablet referring to the fixing of the dry land; but it may belong to a later part of the story, for it is part of a speech to one of the gods. This fragment is—

1. When the foundations of the ground of rock [thou didst make]
2. the foundation of the ground thou didst call . .
3. thou didst beautify the heaven . . . . . .
4. to the face of the heaven . . . . . .
5. thou didst give . . . . . .
6. . . . . . .

There is a second more doubtful fragment which appears to belong to this space, and, like the last, seems to relate part of the creation of the dry land. I give it here under reserve—

1. The god Sar . . . pan . . . .
2. When to the god . . . .

3. Certainly I will cover? . . .

4. from the day that thou . . . .

5. angry thou didst speak . . . .

6. Sar (or Assur) his mouth opened and spake, to the god . . . .

7. Above the sea which is the seat of . . . .

8. in front of the *esara* (firmament?) which I have made . . . .

9. below the place I strengthen it . . . .

10. Let there be made also *e-lu* (earth?) for the dwelling of [man?]

11. Within it his city may he build and . . . .

12. When from the sea he raised . . . .

13. the place . . . . lifted up . . . .

14. above . . . . heaven . . . .

15. the place . . . . lifted up . . . .

16 . . . . Pal-bi-ki the temples of the great gods. . . .

17 . . . . his father and his . . . . of him

18. the god . . . . thee and over all which thy hand has made

19 . . . . thee, having, over the earth which thy hand has made

20 . . . . having, Pal-bi-ki which thou hast called its name

21 . . . . made? my hand for ever

22 . . . . may they carry

23. the place . . . . any one the work which . . .

24. he rejoiced . . . . to after . . . .

25. the gods . . . .

26. which in . . . .

27. he opened . . .

This fragment is both mutilated and obscure; in the eighth line I have translated firmament with a query, the sound and meaning of the word being doubtful; and in line 10, I translate earth for a combination of two characters more obscure still, my translation being a conjecture grounded on some meanings of the individual monograms. Pal-bi-ki are the characters of one name of the city of Assur; but I do not understand the introduction of this name here.

The next recognizable portion of the Creation legends is the upper part of the fifth tablet, which gives the creation of the heavenly bodies, and runs parallel to the account of the fourth day of creation in Genesis.

This tablet opens as follows:—

Fifth Tablet of Creation Legend.

Obverse.

1. It was delightful, all that was fixed by the great gods.

2. Stars, their appearance [in figures] of animals he arranged.

3. To fix the year through the observation of their constellations,

4. twelve months (or signs) of stars in three rows he arranged,

5. from the day when the year commences unto the close.

6. He marked the positions of the wandering stars (planets) to shine in their courses,

7. that they may not do injury, and may not trouble any one,

8. the positions of the gods Bel and Hea he fixed with him.

9. And he opened the great gates in the darkness shrouded

10. the fastenings were strong on the left and right.

11. In its mass (*i.e.* the lower chaos) he made a boiling,

12. the god Uru (the moon) he caused to rise out, the night he overshadowed,

13. to fix it also for the light of the night, until the shining of the day,

14. That the month might not be broken, and in its amount be regular.

15. At the beginning of the month, at the rising of the night,

16. his horns are breaking through to shine on the heaven.

17. On the seventh day to a circle he begins to swell,

18. and stretches towards the dawn further.

19. When the god Shamas (the sun) in the horizon of heaven, in the east,

20. . . . . . formed beautifully and . . . .

21. . . . . . . to the orbit Shamas was perfected

22. . . . . . . .the dawn Shamas should change

23. . . . . going on its path

24. . . . . giving judgment

25. . . . . to tame

26. . . . . a second time

27. . . . .

Reverse.

1. . . . .

2. . . . . . he fixed

3. . . . . of the gods on his hearing.

4. Fifth tablet of "When above" (Creation series).

5. Country of Assurbanipal king of nations king of Assyria.

This fine fragment is a typical specimen of the style of this series, and shows a marked stage in the Creation, the appointment of the heavenly orbs. It parallels the fourth day of Creation in the first chapter of Genesis, where we read: "And God said, Let there be lights in the firmament of the heaven to divide the day from the night; and let them be for signs, and for seasons, and for days, and years:

"15. And let them be for lights in the firmament of the heaven to give light upon the earth: and it was so.

"16. And God made two great lights; the greater light to rule the day, and the lesser light to rule the night; he made the stars also.

"17. And God set them in the firmament of the heaven to give light upon the earth,

"18. And to rule over the day and over the night, and to divide the light from the darkness: and God saw that it was good.

"19. And the evening and the morning were the fourth day."

The fragment of the first tablet of the Creation series showed that that was rather introductory, and dealt with the generation of the gods more than the creation of the universe, and the fact that the fifth tablet contains the Creation given in Genesis, under the fourth day, while a subsequent tablet, probably the seventh, gives the creation of the animals which, according to Genesis, took place on the sixth day, leads to the inference that the events of each of the days of Genesis were recorded on a separate tablet, and that the numbers of the tablets generally followed in the same order as the days of Creation in Genesis, thus:

Genesis, Chap. I.

V. 1 & 2 agree with Tablet 1.

V. 3 to 5 1st day probably with tablet 2.

V. 6 to 8 2nd day probably with tablet 3.

V. 9 to 13 3rd day probably with tablet 4.

V. 14 to 19 4th day agree with tablet 5.

V. 20 to 23 5th day probably with tablet 6.

V. 24 & 25 6th day probably with tablet 7.

V. 26 and following, 6th and 7th day, probably with tablet 8.

The tablet which I think to be the eighth appears to give the Creation and Fall of Man, and is followed by several other tablets giving apparently the war between the gods and the powers of evil, but all of these are very mutilated, and no number can be positively proved beyond the fifth tablet. There is, however, fair reason to suppose that there was a close agreement in subjects and order between the text of the Chaldean legend and Genesis, while there does not appear to be anything like the same agreement between these inscriptions and the accounts transmitted to us through Berosus.

The fifth tablet commences with the statement that the previous creations were "delightful," or satisfactory, agreeing with the oft-repeated statement of Genesis, after each act of creative power, that "God saw that it was good." The only difference here is one of detail. It appears that the Chaldean record contains the review and expression of satisfaction at the head of each tablet, while the Hebrew has it at the close of each act.

We then come to the creation of the heavenly orbs, which are described in the inscription as arranged like animals, while the Bible says they were set as "lights in the firmament of heaven," and just as the book of Genesis says they were set for signs and seasons, for days and years, so the inscription describes that the stars were set in courses to point out the year. The twelve constellations or signs of the zodiac, and two other bands of constellations are mentioned, just as two sets of twelve stars each are mentioned by the Greeks, one north and one south of the zodiac. I have translated one of these names *nibir*, "wandering stars" or "planets," but this is not the usual word for planet, and there is a star called *Nibir* near the place where the sun crossed the boundary between the old and new years, and this star was one of twelve supposed to be favourable to Babylonia. It is evident, from the opening of the inscription on the first tablet of the Chaldean astrology and astronomy, that the functions of the stars were according to the Babylonians to act not only as regulators of the seasons and the year, but to be also used as signs, as in Genesis i. 14, for in those ages it was generally believed that the heavenly bodies gave, by their appearance and positions, signs of events which were coming on the earth.

The passage given in the eighth line of the inscription, to the effect that the God who created the stars fixed places or habitations for Bel and Hea with himself in the heavens, points to the fact that Anu, god of the heavens, was considered to be the creator of the heavenly hosts; for it is he who shares with Bel and Hea the divisions of the face of the sky.

The ninth line of the tablet opens a curious view as to the philosophical beliefs of the early Babylonians. They evidently considered that the world was drawn together out of the waters, and rested or reposed upon a vast abyss of chaotic ocean which filled the space below the world. This dark infernal lake was shut in by gigantic gates and strong fastenings, which prevented the floods from overwhelming the world. When the deity decided to create the moon, he is represented as drawing aside the gates of this abyss, and creating a whirling motion like boiling in the dark ocean below; then, at his bidding, from this turmoil, arose the moon like a giant bubble, and, passing through the open gates, mounted on its destined way across the vaults of heaven.

The Babylonian account continues with the regulation of the motions of the moon to overshadow the night, to regulate and give light until the dawn of day. The phases of the moon are described: its commencing as a thin crescent at the evening on the first day of the month, and its gradually increasing and travelling further into the night. After the moon the creation of the sun is recorded, its beauty and perfection are extolled, and the regularity of its orbit, which led to its being considered the type of a judge, and the regulator of the world.

The Babylonian account of the Creation gives the creation of the moon before that of the sun, in reverse order to that in Genesis, and evidently the Babylonians considered the moon the principal body, while the Book of Genesis makes the sun the greater light. Here it is evident that Genesis is truer to nature than the Chaldean text.

The details of the creation of the planets and stars, which would have been very important to us, are unfortunately lost, no further fragment of this tablet having been recovered.

The colophon at the close of tablet V. gives us, however, part of the first line of the sixth tablet, but not enough to determine its subject. It is probable that this dealt with the creation of creatures of the water and fowls of the air, and that these were the creation of Bel, the companion deity to Anu.

The next tablet, the seventh in the series, is probably represented by a curious fragment, which I first found in one of the trenches at Iiouyunjik, and recognized at once as a part of the description of the Creation.

This fragment is like some of the others, the upper portion of a tablet much broken, and only valuable from its generally clear meaning. The translation of this fragment is:

1. When the gods in their assembly had created . . . . . .
2. were delightful the strong monsters . . . . . .
3. they caused to be living creatures . . . . . .
4. cattle of the field, beasts of the field, and creeping things of the field . . . . . .
5. . . . . they fixed for the living creatures . . . . . .
6. . . . . cattle and creeping things of the city they fixed . . . . . .

7. . . . . . . the assembly of the creeping things the whole which were created . . . . . .

8. . . . . . . which in the assembly of my family . . . . . .

9. . . . . . . and the god Nin-si-ku (the lord of noble face) caused to be two . . . . . .

10 . . . . . . the assembly of the creeping things he caused to go . . . . . .

11. . . . . . . flesh beautiful? . . . . . .

12. . . . . . . pure presence . . . . . .

13. . . . . . . pure presence . . . . . .

---

14. . . . . . . pure presence in the assembly . . .

15 . . . . . .

This tablet corresponds to the sixth day of Creation (Genesis, i. 24–25): "And God said, Let the earth bring forth the living creature after his kind, cattle, and creeping thing, and beast of the earth after his kind: and it was so.

"And God made the beast of the earth after his kind, and cattle after their kind, and everything that creepeth upon the earth after his kind: and God saw that it was good."

The Assyrian tablet commences with a statement of the satisfaction a former creation, apparently that of the monsters or whales, had given; here referring to Genesis i. 23. It then goes on to relate the creating of living animals on land, three kinds being distinguished, exactly agreeing with the Genesis account, and then we have in the ninth line a curious but broken account of Nin-si-ku (one of the names of Hea), creating two beings to be with the animals, the wording of the next fragmentary lines leading to the suspicion that this was the opening of the account of the creation of man. This, however, is only a suspicion, for the lines are so mutilated and obscure that nothing can be fairly proved from them. It is curious here, however, to notice a tablet which refers to the creation of man. In this tablet, K 63, the creation of the human race is given to Hea, and all the references in other inscriptions make this his work.

In considering the next fragments, those which really relate to man, there is great difficulty; for, in the first fragment to be noticed, on one side the mutilation of the tablet renders the sense totally uncertain; in the space lost there may be a string of negatives which would entirely reverse the meaning. It is probable that the other side of the fragment is a discourse to the first woman on her duties.

I think it to be the reverse of the tablet which, so far as it can be translated, appears to give the speech of the deity to the newly created pair (man and woman) instructing them in their duties.

K 3364 obverse.

(Many lines lost.)

1. evil . . . .
2. which is eaten by the stomach . . . .
3. in growing . . . .
4. consumed . . . .
5. extended, heavy, ...
6. firmly thou shalt speak . . . .
7. and the support of mankind . . . thee
8. Every day thy god thou shalt approach (or invoke)
9. sacrifice, prayer of the mouth and instruments . . . . . .
10. to thy god in reverence thou shalt carry.
11. Whatever shall be suitable for divinity,
12. supplication, humility, and bowing of the face,
13. fire? thou shalt give to him, and thou shalt bring tribute,
14. and in the fear also of god thou shalt be holy.
15. In thy knowledge and afterwards in the tablets (writing)
16. worship and goodness . . . shall be raised?
17. Sacrifice saving . . . .
18. and worship . . . .
19. the fear of god thou shalt not leave . . . .
20. the fear of the angels thou shalt live in . . . .
21. With friend and enemy? speech thou shalt make? . . . .
22. under? speech thou shalt make good . . . .
23. When thou shalt speak also he will give . . . .
24. When thou shalt trust also thou . . . .
25. to enemy? also . . . .
26. . . . thou shalt trust a friend . . . .
27. . . . thy knowledge also

Reverse.

(Many lines lost.)

1. Beautiful place also . . . . divide . . . .
2. in beauty and . . . . thy hand . . . .
3. and thou to the presence . . . . thou shalt fix . . .
4. and not thy sentence . . . . thee to the end?

5. in the presence of beauty and . . . . thou shalt speak
6. of thy beauty and . . . .
7. beautiful and . . . . to give drink?
8. circle I fill? his enemies
9. his rising? he seeks . . . . the man . . . .
10. with the lord of thy beauty thou shalt be faithful,
11. to do evil thou shalt not approach him,
12. at thy illness . . . . to him
13. at thy distress . . . .

The obverse of this tablet is a fragment of the address from the deity to the newly created man on his duties to his god, and it is curious that while, in other parts of the story, various gods are mentioned by name, here only one god is mentioned, and simply as the "God." The fragments of this tablet might belong to the purest system of religion; but it would in this case be wrong to ground an argument on a single fragment.

The reverse of the tablet appears, so far as the sense can be ascertained, to be addressed to the woman, the companion of the man, informing her of her duties towards her partner.

The next fragment is a small one; it is the lower corner of a tablet with the ends of a few lines. It may possibly belong to the tablet of the Fall to be mentioned later.

This fragment is of importance, small as it is, because it mentions a speech of Hea to man, and alludes to the Karkartiamat, or dragon of the sea, in connection with a revolt against the deity. The fragment is, however, too mutilated to give more than a general idea of its contents.

Obverse.
1. . . . . . seat her
2. . . . . . all the lords
3. . . . . . his might
4. . . . . . the gods, lord lofty?
5. . . . . kingdom exalted
6. . . . . . in multitudes increase
Reverse.
1. . . . . . Hea called to his man
2. . . . . . height of his greatness
3. . . . . . the rule of any god
4. . . . . . Sartulku knew it
5. . . . . . his noble . . . .

6. . . . . his fear? Sartulku

7. . . . . his might

8. . . . . to them, the dragon of the sea

9. . . . . against thy father fight

Connected with this fragment is the account of the curse after the Fall, on the remarkable fragment which I brought over from my first expedition to Assyria.

This forms about half a tablet, being part of the obverse and reverse, both in fair preservation; and so far as they go, fairly perfect, but containing at present many obscurities in the speeches of the gods. Before the commencement of lines 1, 5, 11, 19, 27, and 29 on the obverse, there are glosses stating that the divine titles commencing these lines all apply to the same deity. These explanatory glosses show that even in the Assyrian time there were difficulties in the narrative.

Obverse.

1. The god Zi . . . . .

2. which he had fixed . . . . .

3. their account . . . . .

4. may not fail in preparing? . . . . .

5. The god Ziku (Noble life) quickly called; Director of purity,

6. good kinsman, master of perception and right,

7. causer to be fruitful and abundant, establisher of fertility,

8. another to us has come up, and greatly increased,

9. in thy powerful advance spread over him good,

10. may he speak, may he glorify, may he exalt his majesty.

11. The god Mir-ku (noble crown) in concern, raised a protection?

12. lord of noble lips, saviour from death

13. of the gods imprisoned, the accomplisher of restoration,

14. his pleasure he established he fixed upon the gods his enemies,

15. to fear them he made man,

16. the breath of life was in him.

17. May he be established, and may his will not fail,

18. in the mouth of the dark races which his hand has made.

19. The god of noble lips with his five fingers sin may he cut off;

20. who with his noble charms removes the evil curse.

21. The god Libzu wise among the gods, who had chosen his possession,

22. the doing of evil shall not come out of him,

23. established in the company of the gods, he rejoices their heart.

24. Subduer of the unbeliever . . . . .
25. director of right . . . . .
26. of corruption and . . . . .
27. The god Nissi . . . . .
28. keeper of watch . . . . .
29. The god Suhhab, swiftly . . . . .
30. the pourer out to them . . . . .
31. in . . . . .
32. like . . .
33 . . . . .
Reverse.
1. . . . . .
2. . . . . . the star . . . . .
3. may he take the tail and head . . . . .
4. because the dragon Tiamat had . . . . .
5. his punishment the planets possessing . . . .
6. by the stars of heaven themselves may they . .
7. like a sheep may the gods tremble all of them
8. may he bind Tiamat her prisons may he shut up and surround.
9. Afterwards the people of remote ages
10. may she remove, not destroy . . . for ever,
11. to the place he created, he made strong.
12. Lord of the earth his name called out, the father Elu
13. in the ranks of the angels pronounced their curse.
14. The god Hea heard and his liver was angry,
15. because his man had corrupted his purity.
16. He like me also Hea may he punish him,
17. the course of my issue all of them may he remove, and
18. all my seed may he destroy.
19. In the language of the fifty great gods
20. by his fifty names he called, and turned away in anger from him:
21. May he be conquered, and at once cut off.
22. Wisdom and knowledge hostilely may they injure him.
23. May they put at enmity also father and son and may they plunder.
24. to king, ruler, and governor, may they bend their ear.
25. May they cause anger also to the lord of the gods Merodach.
26. His land may it bring forth but he not touch it;
27. his desire shall be cut off, and his will be unanswered;

28. the opening of his mouth no god shall take notice of;

29. his back shall be broken and not be healed;

30. at his urgent trouble no god shall receive him;

31. his heart shall be poured out, and his mind shall be troubled;

32. to sin and wrong his face shall come . . . . .

33. . . . . . front . . . . .

34. . . . . . .

In a second copy which presents several variations lines 14 to 19 are omitted.

This valuable fragment is unfortunately obscure in some parts, especially on the obverse, but the general meaning is undoubted, and the approximate position of the fragment in the story is quite clear. It evidently follows the fragment giving the creation of the land animals, and either forms a further portion of the same, or part of the following tablet.

The obverse gives a series of speeches and statements respecting the newly created man, who was supposed to be under the especial care of the deities. It happens in this case that there is no clue to the reason for these speeches, the key portions of the inscription being lost, but a point is evidently made of the purity of the man, who is said to be established in the company of the gods and to rejoice their hearts. The various divine titles or names, "the god of noble life," "the god of noble crown," and "the god of noble lips," are all most probably titles of Hea.

It appears from line 18 that the race of human beings spoken of is the *zalmat-qaqadi*, or dark race, and in various other fragments of these legends they are called Admi or Adami, which is exactly the name given to the first man in Genesis.

The word Adam used in these legends for the first human being is evidently not a proper name, but is only used as a term for mankind. Adam appears as a proper name in Genesis, but certainly in some passages is only used in the same sense as the Assyrian word, and we are told on the creation of human beings (Genesis, v. 1): "In the day that God created man, in the likeness of God made he him; male and female created he them; and blessed them, and called their name Adam, in the day when they were created."

It has already been pointed out by Sir Henry Rawlinson that the Babylonians recognized two principal races: the Adamu, or dark race, and the Sarku, or light race, probably in the same manner that two races are mentioned in Genesis, the sons of Adam and the sons of God. It appears incidentally . from the fragments of inscriptions that it was the race of Adam, or the dark race, which was believed to have fallen, but there is at present no clue to the position of the other race in their system. We are informed in Genesis that when the world became corrupt the sons of God intermarried with the race of Adam, and thus spread the evils which had commenced with the Adamites (see Genesis, ch. vi.).

The obverse of the tablet giving the creation of man, where it breaks off leaves him in a state of purity, and where the narrative recommences on the reverse man has already fallen.

Here it is difficult to say how far the narrative of the inscription agrees with that of the Bible. In this case it is better to review the Biblical account, which is complete, and compare it with the fragmentary allusions in the inscriptions.

After the statement of man's innocence, which agrees with the inscription, the Bible goes on to relate (Genesis, iii. 1), that the serpent was more subtle than any beast of the field, and that he tempted the woman to sin. This attributes the origin of sin to the serpent, but nothing whatever is said as to the origin or history of the serpent. The fragmentary account of the Fall in the inscriptions mentions the dragon Tiamat, or the dragon of the sea, evidently in the same relation as the serpent, being concerned in bringing about the Fall. This dragon is called the dragon of tiamat or the sea; it is generally conceived of as a griffin, and is connected with the original chaos, the Thalatth of Berosus, the female principle which, according to both the inscriptions and Berosus, existed before the creation of the universe. This was the original spirit of chaos and disorder, a spirit opposed in principle to the gods, and, according to the Babylonians, self-existent and eternal, older even than the gods, for the birth or separation of the deities out of this chaos was the first step in the creation of the world.

According to Genesis, the serpent addressed the woman (Genesis, iii. 1), and inquired if God had forbidden them to eat of every tree of the Garden of Eden, eliciting from her the statement that there was a tree in the middle of the Garden, the fruit of which was forbidden to them. There is nothing in the present fragments indicating a belief in the Garden of Eden or the Tree of Knowledge; there is only an obscure allusion in lines 16 and 22 to a thirst for knowledge having been a cause of man's fall, but outside these inscriptions, from the general body of Assyrian texts, Sir Henry Rawlinson has pointed out the agreement of the Babylonian region of Karduniyas or Ganduniyas with the Eden of the Bible. Eden is a fruitful place, watered by the four rivers, Euphrates, Tigris, Gihon, and Pison, and Ganduniyas is similar in description, watered by the four rivers, Euphrates, Tigris, Surappi, and Ukni. The loss of this portion of the Creation legend is unfortunate, as, however probable it may be that the Hebrew and Babylonian traditions agree about the Garden and Tree of Knowledge, we cannot now prove it. There is a second tree, the Tree of Life, in the Genesis account (ch. iii. 22), which certainly appears to correspond to the sacred grove of Anu, which a later fragment states was guarded by a sword turning to all the four points of the compass.

In several other places in the Genesis legends, and especially in the legends of Izdubar, there are allusions to the tree, grove, or forest of the gods, and this divine tree or grove is often represented on the sculptures, both in the Babylonian gem engravings, and on the walls of the Assyrian palaces and temples. When the representation is complete, the tree is attended by two figures of cherubims, one on each side of the sacred emblem.

According to Genesis, Adam and Eve, tempted by the serpent, eat of the fruit of the Tree of Knowledge, and so by disobedience brought sin into the world. These details are also lost in the cuneiform text, which opens again where the gods are cursing the dragon and the Adam or man for this transgression, corresponding to the passage, Genesis, iii. 9 to 19. Throughout this, corresponding passages may be found which show that the same idea runs through both narratives, but some passages in the cuneiform account are too mutilated to allow any certainty to be attached to the translation, and the loss of the previous parts of the text prevents our knowing what points the allusions are directed to.

Although so much of the most important part of the text is lost, the notices in other parts, and the allusions in the mythological scenes on the Babylonian gems will serve to guide us as to the probable drift of the missing portion.

It is quite clear that the dragon of the sea or dragon of Tiamat is connected with the Fall like the serpent in the book of Genesis, and in fact is the equivalent of the serpent. The name of the dragon is not written phonetically, but by two monograms which probably mean the "scaly one," or animal covered with scales. This description, of course, might apply either to a fabulous dragon, a serpent, or a fish.

The only passage where there is any phonetic explanation of the signs is in "Cuneiform Inscriptions," vol. ii. p. 32, l. 9, where we have *turbuhtu* for the place or den of the dragon, perhaps connected with the Hebrew בחר, sea-monster. The form of this creature as given on the gems is that of a griffin or dragon generally with a head like a carnivorous animal, body covered with scales, legs terminating in claws, like an eagle, and wings on the back. Our own heraldic griffins are so strikingly like the sculptures of this creature that we might almost suspect them to be copies from the Chaldean works. In some cases, however, the early Babylonian seals, which contained devices taken from these legends, more closely approached the Genesis story. One striking and important specimen of early type in the British Museum collection has two figures sitting one on each side of a tree, holding out their hands to the fruit, while at the back of one is stretched a serpent. We know well that in these early sculptures none of these figures were chance devices, but all represented events or supposed events, and figures in their legends; thus it is evident that a form of the story of the Fall, similar to that of Genesis, was known in early times in Babylonia.

The dragon which, in the Chaldean account of the Creation, leads man to sin, is the creature of Tiamat, the living principle of the sea and of chaos, and he is an embodiment of the spirit of chaos or disorder which was opposed to the deities at the creation of the world.

It is clear that the dragon is included in the curse for the Fall, and that the gods invoke on the head of the human race all the evils which afflict humanity. Wisdom and knowledge shall injure him (line 22), he shall have family quarrels (line 23), shall submit to tyranny (line 24), he will anger the gods (line 25), he shall not eat the fruit of his labour (line 26), he shall be disappointed in his desires (line 27), he shall pour out useless prayer (lines 28 and 30), he shall have trouble of mind and body (lines 29 and 31), he shall commit future sin (line 32). No doubt subsequent lines continue these topics, but again our narrative is broken, and it only reopens where the gods are preparing for war with the powers of evil, which are led by Tiamat, which war probably arose from the part played by Tiamat in the fall of man.

My first idea of this part was that the war with the powers of evil preceded the Creation; I now think it followed the account of the Fall, but I have no direct proof of this.

Of the subsequent tablets of this series, which include the war between the gods and powers of evil, and the punishment of the dragon Tiamat, there are several fragments.

The first of these is K 4832, too mutilated to translate, it contains speeches of the gods before the war.

The second fragment, K 3473, contains also speeches, and shows the gods preparing for battle. It is very fragmentary.

1. . . . . his mouth opened
2. . . . . his . . a word he spoke
3. . . . . satisfy my anger
4. . . . . of thee let me send to thee
5. . . . . thou ascendest
6. . . . . thee to thy presence
7. . . . . their curse
8. . . . . in a circle may they sit
9. . . . . let them make the vine?
10. . . . . of them may they hear the renown
11. . . . . cover them he set and
12. . . . . thee change to them
13. . . . . he sent me
14. . . . . he held me
15. . . . . he sinned against me
16. . . . . and angrily . . . .
17. . . . . the gods all of them
18. . . . . made her hands . . . .
19. . . . . and his hand Tiamat coming
20. . . . . destroyed not night and day
21. . . . . burning . . .
22. . . . . they made division
23. . . . . the end of all hands
24. . . . . formerly thou . . . great serpents
25. . . . . unyielding I . . . .
26. . . . . their bodies fill . . . .
27. . . . . fear shall cover them
(Several other mutilated lines.)

The third fragment, K 3938, is on the same subject; some lines of this give the following general meaning:—

1. great animal . . . .
2. fear he made to carry . . . .
3. their sight was very great . . . .
4. their bodies were powerful and . . . .

5. . . . . delightful, strong serpent . . . .
6. Udgallu, Urbat and . . . .
7. days arranged, five . . . .
8. carrying weapons unyielding . . . .
9. her breast, her back . . . .
10. flowing? and first . . . .
11. among the gods collected . . . .
12. the god Kingu subdued . . . .
13. marching in front before . . . .
14. carrying weapons thou . . . .
15. upon war . . . .
16. his hand appointed

There are many more similar broken lines, and on the other side fragments of a speech by some being who desires Tiamat to make war.

All these fragments are not sufficiently complete to translate with certainty, or even to ascertain their order.

The fourth fragment, K 3449, relates to the making of weapons to arm the god who should meet in war the dragon.

This reads with some doubt on account of its mutilation:
1. heart . . . . .
2. burning . . . . .
3. from . . . . .
4. in the temple . . . . .
5. may he fix . . . . .
6. the dwelling of the god . . . . .
7. the great gods . . . . .
8. the gods said? . . . . .
9. the sword that was made the gods saw
10. and they saw also the bow which was strung . . . . .
11. the work that was made they placed . . . . .
12. carried also Anu in the assembly of the gods . . . . .
13. the bow he fitted she . . . . .
14. and he spake of the bow thus and said
15. Noble wood who shall first thus draw thee? against?
16. speed her punishment the star of the bow in heaven . . . . .
17. and establish the resting place of . . . . .
18. from the choice of . . . . .
19. and place his throne . . . . .

20. . . . . . in heaven . . . . .

21. . . . . . .

The next fragment or collection of fragments gives the final struggle between Tiamat and Merodach or Bel, and this fragment appears to distinguish between the dragon of Tiamat or the sea monster, and Tiamat the female personification of the sea; but I am not sure of this distinction. The *saparu*, or sickle-shaped sword, is always represented both in the sculptures and inscriptions as a weapon of Bel in this war.

Sixth Fragment.

1. . . . . he fixed . . . .

2. . . . . to his right hand he distributed

p. 96

3. . . . . and quiver his hand hurled,

4. the lightning he sent before him,

5. . . . . fierceness filled his body.

6. He made the sword to silence the dragon of the sea,

7. the seven winds he fixed not to come out of her wound.

8. On the South, the North, the East, and the West,

9. his hand the sword he caused to hold before the grove of his father the god Anu.

10. He made the evil wind, the hostile wind, the tempest, the storm,

11. the four winds, the seven winds, the wind of . . . ., the irregular wind.

12. He brought out the winds he had created seven-of them,

13. the dragon of the sea stretched out, came after him,

14. he carried the thunderbolt his great weapon,

15. in a chariot . . . unrivalled, driving he rode:

16. he took her and four fetters on her hands he fastened,

17. . . . . unyielding, storming . . . . her

18. . . . . with their sting bringing death

19. . . . . sweeping away knowledge

20. . . . . destruction and fighting

21. . . . . left hand . . . .

22. . . . . fear . . . .

(Several other fragmentary lines.)

Reverse.

1. . . . . . . the god Sar . . . . .

2. . . . . . . dwelling . . . . .

3. . . . . . before the weapon . . . . .
4. . . . . . field . . . . .
5. . . . . . above . . . . .
6. . . . . . struck to the god . . . . .
7. . . . . . them . . . . .
8. . . . . . cut into . . . . .
9. . . . . . said to his wife . . . . .
10. . . . . . him to break the god . . . . .
11. . . . . . evil? thou shalt be delivered and . . . . .
12. . . . . . thy evil thou shalt subdue,
13. the tribute to thy maternity shall be forced upon them by thy weapons,
14. I will stand by and to thee they shall be made a spoil.
15. Tiamat on hearing this
16. at once joined and changed her resolution.
17. Tiamat called and quickly arose,
18. strongly and firmly she encircled with her defences,
19. she took a girdle? and placed . . . . .
20. and the gods for war prepared for them their weapons.
21. Tiamat attacked the just prince of the gods Merodach,
22. the standards they raised in the conflict like a battle.
23. Bel also drew out his sword and wounded her.
24. The evil wind coming afterwards struck against her face.
25. Tiamat opened her mouth to swallow him,
26. the evil wind he caused to enter, before she could shut her lips;
27. the force of the wind her stomach filled, and
28. her heart trembled, and her face was distorted,
29. . . . . . violently seized her stomach,
30. her inside it broke, and conquered her heart.
31. He imprisoned her, and her work he ended.
32. Her allies stood over her astonished,
33. when Tiamat their leader was conquered.
34. Her ranks he broke, her assembly was scattered,
35. and the gods her helpers who went beside her
36. trembled, feared, and broke up themselves,
37. the expiring of her life they fled from,
38. war surrounding they were fleeing not standing?
39. . . . . . them and their weapons he broke

40. like a sword cast down, sitting in darkness,

41. knowing their capture, full of grief,

42. their strength removed, shut in bonds,

43. and at once the strength of their work was overcome with terror,

44. the throwing of stones going . . . .

45. He cast down the enemy, his hand . . . .

46. part of the enemy under him . . . .

47. and the god Kingu again . . . .

48. . . . .

Again the main difficulty arises from the fragmentary state of the documents, it being impossible even to decide the order of the fragments. It appears, however, that the gods have fashioned for them a sword and a bow to fight the dragon Tiamat, and Anu proclaims great honour (fourth fragment, lines 15 to 20) to any of the gods who will engage in battle with her. Bel or Merodach volunteers, and goes forth armed with these weapons to fight the dragon. Tiamat is encouraged by one of the gods who has become her husband, and meets Merodach in battle. The description of the fight and the subsequent triumph of the god are very fine, and remarkably curious in their details, but the connection between the fragments is so uncertain at present that it is better to reserve comment upon them until the text is more complete. This war between the powers of good and evil, chaos and order, is extra to the Creation, does not correspond with anything in Genesis, but rather finds its parallel in the war between Michael and the dragon in Revelation, xii. 7 to 9, where the dragon is called "the great dragon, that old serpent, called the devil and Satan, which deceiveth the whole world." This description is strikingly like the impression gathered from the fragments of the cuneiform story; the dragon Tiamat who fought against the gods and led man to sin, and whose fate it was to be conquered in a celestial war, closely corresponds in all essential points to the dragon conquered by Michael. These fragments of the cuneiform account of the Creation and Fall agree so far as they are preserved with the Biblical account, and show that in the period from B.C. 2000 to 1500 the Babylonians believed in a similar story to that in Genesis.

CHAPTER VI: OTHER BABYLONIAN ACCOUNTS OF THE CREATION.

Cuneiform accounts originally traditions.—Variations.—Account of Berosus.—Tablet from Cutha.—Translation.—Composite animals.—Eagle-headed men.—Seven brothers.—Destruction of men.—Seven wicked spirits.—War in heaven.—Variations of story.—Poetical account of Creation.

IN the last chapter I have given the fragments of the principal story of the Creation and Fall from the cuneiform inscriptions, but it appears from the tablets that all these legends were "traditions" or "stories" repeated by word of mouth, and afterwards committed to writing. When such traditions are not reduced to writing, and depend on being handed down from generation to generation by word of mouth, they are liable to vary, sometimes very widely, according to the period and condition of the country. Thus many different versions of a story arise, and there can be no doubt that this was actually the case with the Creation legends. There must have been a belief in the Creation and some of the leading features of this story long before these Creation legends were committed to writing, and there is evidence of other stories, related to those already given, which were at about the same time committed to writing. The story of the Creation transmitted through Berosus (see chapter iii. pp. 37–50) supplies us with a totally different story, differing entirely from the cuneiform account in the last chapter and from the Genesis account, and some fragments of tablets from Kouyunjik belonging to the library of Assurbanipal give a copy, mutilated as usual, of another version having many points of agreement with the account of Berosus. This legend, of which the following is a translation, is stated to be copied from a tablet at Cutha.

Legend of Creation from Cutha tablet.
(Many lines lost at commencement.)
1. lord of . . . .
2. . . . . his lord the strength of the gods . . . .
3. . . . . his host . . . . host . . . .
4. lord of the upper region and the lower region lord of angels . . . .

5. who drank turbid waters and pure water did not drink,

6. with his flame, his weapon, that man he enclosed,

7. . . . . he took, he destroyed,

8. on a tablet nothing was then written, and there were not left the carcasses and waste?

9. from the earth nothing arose and I had not come to it.

10. Men with the bodies of birds of the desert, human beings

11. with the faces of ravens,

12. these the great gods created,

13. and in the earth the gods created for them a dwelling.

14. Tamat gave unto them strength,

15. their life the mistress of the gods raised,

16. in the midst of the earth they grew up and became great,

17. and increased in number,

18. Seven kings brothers of the same family,

19. six thousand in number were their people,

20. Banini their father was king, their mother

21. the queen was Milili,

22. their eldest brother who went before them, Mimangab was his name,

23. their second brother Mididu was his name,

24. their third brother . . . . tur was his name,

25. their fourth brother . . . . dada was his name,

26. their fifth brother . . . . tah was his name,

27. their sixth brother . . . . ru was his name,

28. their seventh brother . . . . was his name.

COLUMN II.

(Many lines lost.)

1. . . . . . evil . . . .

2. man his will turned

3. in . . . . I purified?

4. On a tablet the evil curse of man he carved?

5. I called the worshippers and sent,

6. seven in width and seven in depth I arranged them.

7. I gave them noble reeds? (pipes?)

8. I worshipped also the great gods

9. Ishtar, ..., Zamama, Anunitu

10. Nebo . . . . Shamas the warrior,

11. the gods listened to my doings

12. . . . . he did not give and
13. thus I said in my heart:
14. Now here am I and
15. let there not . . . . ground
16. let . there not . . . .
17. may I go as I trust in Bel . . . . my heart,
18. and . . . . my iron may I take.
19. In the first year in the course of it
20. one hundred and twenty thousand men I sent out and among them,
21. one of them did not return.
22. In the second year in the course of it, ninety thousand the same.
23. In the third year in the course of it, sixty thousand seven hundred the same.
24. They were rooted out they were punished, I eat,
25. I rejoiced, I made a rest.
26. Thus I said in my heart now here am I and
27. at this time what is left?
28. I the king, am not the preserver of his country,
29. and the ruler is not the preserver of his people.
30. When I have done may corpses and waste be left,
31. the saving of the people from night, death, spirits, curses,
(Many more broken lines, meaning quite uncertain.)
FRAGMENT OF COLUMN III.
1. . . . . I caused to pursue . . . .
2. . . . . . blood . . . .
3. in the midst of them twelve men fled from me.
4. After them I pursued, swiftly I went,
5. those men, I captured them
6. those men I turned . . . . .
7. Thus I said in my heart . . . . .
COLUMN IV.
(Several lines lost at commencement.)
1. to . . . . .
2. the powerful king . . . .
3. the gods . . . .
4. hand . . . . take them
5. thou king, viceroy, prince, or any one else,
6. whom God shall call, and who shall rule the kingdom,

7. who shall rebuild this house, this tablet I write to thee,

8. in the city of Cutha, in the temple of Sitlam,

9. in the sanctuary of Nergal, I leave for thee;

10. this tablet see, and,

11. to the words of this tablet listen, and

12. do not rebel, do not fail,

13. do not fear, and do not turn away,

14. then may thy support be established,

15. thou in thy works shall be glorious,

16. thy forts shall be strong,

17. thy canals shall be full of water,

18. thy treasures, thy corn, thy silver,

19. thy furniture, thy goods,

20. and thy instruments, shall be multiplied.

(A few more mutilated lines.)

This is a very obscure inscription, the first column, however, forms part of a relation similar to that of Berosus in his history of the Creation; the beings who were killed by the light, and those with men's heads and bird's bodies, and bird's heads and men's bodies, agree with the composite monsters of Berosus, while the goddess of chaos, Tiamat, who is over them, is the same again as the Tiamat of the Creation legends and the Thalatth of Berosus.

The relation in the second and third columns of the inscription is difficult, and does not correspond with any known incident. The fourth column contains an address to any future king who should read the inscription which was deposited in the temple of Nergal at Cutha.

It is probable that this legend was supposed to be the work of one of the mythical kings of Chaldea, who describes the condition and history of the world before his time.

There is another legend which appears to be connected with these, the legend of the seven evil spirits, which I have given in my former work, "Assyrian Discoveries," p. 398.

Tablet with the story of the Seven Wicked Gods or Spirits.

COLUMN I.

1. In the first days the evil gods

2. the angels who were in rebellion, who in the lower part of heaven

3. had been created,

4. they caused their evil work

5. devising with wicked heads . . .

6. ruling to the river . . . .

7. There were seven of them. The first was . . .

8. the second was a great animal . . . .

9. . . . . which any one . . . .

10. the third was a leopard . . . .

11. the fourth was a serpent . . . .

12. the fifth was a terrible . . . . which to . . . .

13. the sixth was a striker which to god and king did not submit,

14. the seventh was the messenger of the evil wind which . . . . made.

15. The seven of them messengers of the god Anu their king

16. from city to city went round

17. the tempest of heaven was strongly bound to them,

18. the flying clouds of heaven surrounded them,

19. the downpour of the skies which in the bright day

20. makes darkness, was attached to them

21. with a violent wind, an evil wind, they began,

22. the tempest of Vul was their might,

23. at the right hand of Vul they came,

24. from the surface of heaven like lightning they darted,

25. descending to the abyss of waters, at first they came.

26. In the wide heavens of the god Anu the king

27. evil they set up, and an opponent they had not.

28. At this time Bel of this matter heard and

29. the account sank into his heart.

30. With Hea the noble sage of the gods he took counsel, and

31. Sin (the moon), Shamas (the sun), and Ishtar (Venus) in the lower part of heaven to control it he appointed.

32. With Anu to the government of the whole of heaven he set them up.

33. To the three of them the gods his children,

34. day and night to be united and not to break apart,

35. he urged them.

36. In those days those seven evil spirits

37. in the lower part of heaven commencing,

38. before the light of Sin fiercely they came,

39. the noble Shamas and Vul (the god of the atmosphere) the warrior to their side they turned and

40. Ishtar with Anu the king into a noble seat

41. they raised and in the government of heaven they fixed.

COLUMN II.

1. The god . . . . .
2. . . . . .
3. The god . . . . .
4. which . . . . .
5. In those days the seven of them . . . .
6. at the head in the control to . . . . .
7. evil . . . . .
8. for the drinking of his noble mouth . . . .
9. The god Sin the ruler . . . . mankind
10. . . . . . . of the earth
11. . . . . . . troubled and on high he sat,
12. night and day fearing, in the seat of his dominion he did not sit.
13. Those evil gods the messengers of Anu their king
14. devised with wicked heads to assist one another, and
15. evil they spake together, and
16. from the midst of heaven like a wind to the earth they carne down.
17. The god Bel of the noble Sin, his trouble
18. in heaven, he saw and
19. Bel to his attendant the god Nusku said:
20. "Attendant Nusku this account to the ocean carry, and
21. the news of my child Sin who in heaven is greatly troubled;
22. to the god Hea in the ocean repeat."
23. Nusku the will of his lord obeyed, and
24. to Hea in the ocean descended and went.
25. To the prince, the noble sage, the lord, the god unfailing,
26. Nusku the message of his lord at once repeated.
27. Hea in the ocean that message heard, and
28. his lips spake, and with wisdom his mouth was filled.
29. Hea his son the god Merodach called, and this word he spake
30. "Go my son Merodach
31. enter into the shining Sin who in heaven is greatly troubled;
32. his trouble from heaven expel.
33. Seven of them the evil gods, spirits of death, having no fear,
34. seven of them the evil gods, who like a flood
35. descend and sweep over the earth.
36. To the earth like a storm they come down.

37. Before the light of Sin fiercely they came

38. the noble Shamas and Vul the warrior, to their side they turned and . .
. .

The end of this legend is lost; it probably recorded the interference of Merodach in favour of Sin, the moon god.

In this story, which differs again from all the others, Bel is supposed to place in the heaven the Moon, Sun, and Venus, the representative of the stars. The details have no analogy with the other stories, and this can only be considered a poetical myth of the Creation.

This legend is part of the sixteenth tablet of the series on evil spirits; but the tablet contains other matters as well, the legend apparently being only quoted in it. There is another remarkable legend of the same sort on another tablet of this series published in "Cuneiform Inscriptions," vol. iv. p. 15. The whole of this series concerns the wanderings of the god Merodach, who goes about the world seeking to remove curses and spells, and in every difficulty applying to his father Hea to learn how to combat the influence of the evil spirits, to whom all misfortunes were attributed.

CHAPTER VII: THE SIN OF THE GOD ZU.

God Zu.—Obscurity of legend.—Translation.—Sin of Zu.—Anger of
the gods.—Speeches of Anu to Vul.—Vul's answer.—Speech of Anu to
Nebo.—Answer of Nebo.—Sarturda.—Changes to a bird.—The Zu
bird.—Bird of prey.—Sarturda lord of Amarda.

AMONG the legends of the gods, companion stories to the accounts of
the Creation and Deluge, one of the most curious is the legend of the sin
committed by the god Zu.

This legend stands alone among the stories, its incidents and its principal
actor being otherwise almost unknown from cuneiform sources. I have at
present only detected one copy of the story, and this is in so mutilated a
condition that it cannot be connected with any other of the legends. From
some similarity in style, I conjecture that it may form the first tablet of the
series which I have termed the "Wars of the Gods." I have, however, no
sufficient evidence to connect the two, and for this reason give it here a
separate place, preceding the tablets of the "Wars of the Gods."

The principal actor in the legend is a being named Zu, the name being
found in all three cases of an Assyrian noun Zu, Za and Zi. Preceding the
name is the determinative of divinity, from which I judge Zu to have been
ranked among the gods.

The story of the sin of Zu has sometimes reminded me of the outrage of
Ham on his father Noah, and the mutilation of Ouranus by his son Saturn,
but there is not sufficient evidence to connect the stories, and there are in
the Assyrian account several very difficult words. One of these is
particularly obscure, and I only transcribe it here by the ordinary phonetic
values of the characters *um-sim-i*, it may possibly mean some talisman or
oracle in the possession of Bel, which was robbed from him by Zu. There
are besides the two difficult words *parzi* and *tereti*, which I have preferred
merely transcribing in my translation. It must be added that the inscription
is seriously mutilated in some parts, giving additional difficulty in the
translation.

The tablet containing the account of the sin of Zu, K 3454, in the
Museum collection, originally contained four columns of text, each column

having about sixty lines of writing. The first and fourth column are almost entirely lost, there not being enough anywhere to translate from.

The single fragment preserved, belonging to the first column, mentions some being who was the seed or firstborn of Elu or Bel, with a number of titles, such as "warrior, soldier of the temple of Hamsi," and the name of the god Zu occurs, but not so as to prove these titles to be his.

The following is a partial translation of the remains of this tablet:—

K. 3454.

COLUMN I. lost.

COLUMN II.

1. the fate? going . . . . of the gods all of them he sent.

2. . . . . Zu grew old and

3. Zu? like . . . . Bel . . . . him

4. three? streams? of water in front and

5. the work Bel finished? he slept in it.

6. The crown of his majesty, the clothing of his divinity,

7. his *umsimi*, his crown? Zu stripped, and

8. he stripped also the father of the gods, the venerable of heaven and earth.

9. The desire? of majesty he conceived in his heart,

10. Zu stripped also the father of the gods, the venerable of heaven and earth.

11. The desire? of majesty he conceived in his heart:

12. Let me carry away the *umsimi* of the gods,

13. and the *tereti* of all the gods may it burn,

14. may my throne be established, may I possess the *parzi*,

15. may I govern the whole of the seed of the angels.

16. And he hardened his heart to make war,

17. in the vicinity of the house where he slept, he waited until the head of the day.

18. When Bel poured out the beautiful waters

19. spread out on the seat his crown? was placed,

20. the *umsimi* he took in his hand,

21. the majesty he carried off; he cast away the *parzi*,

22. Zu fled away and in his country concealed himself.

23. Then spread darkness, and made a commotion,

24. the father, their king, the ruler Bel.

25. . . . . . he sent the glory of the gods

26. divinity was destroyed in . . . .
27. Anu his mouth opened, and spake
28. and said to the gods his sons:
29. Whoever will, let him slay Zu,
30. in all the countries may his name be renowned.

---

31. To Vul the powerful light the son of Anu
32. a speech he made to him, also and spake to him.
33. To Vul the powerful light the son of Anti
34. a speech he made to him, also and spake to him:
35. Hero Vul let there not be opposition in thee
36. slay Zu with thy weapon.
37. May thy name be renowned in the assembly of the gods,
38. in the midst of thy brothers, first set up,
39. . . . . made also fragrant with spices,
40. in the four regions they shall fix thy city.
41. May thy city be exalted like the temple,
42. they shall cry in the presence of the gods and praise thy name.
43. Vul answered the speech,
44. to his father Anu word he spake;
45. Father to a desert country do thou consign him.
46. Let Zu not come among the gods thy sons,
47. for the *umsimi* he took in his hand,
48. the majesty he carried off, he cast away the *parzi*,
49. and Zu fled away and in his country concealed himself.
50. . . . . . . opening his mouth like the venerable of heaven and earth
51. . . . . like mud
52. . . . . . . was, the gods swept away
53. . . . . . . I will not go he said.

(Sixteen lines lost here, part on this column, part on Column III.)
COLUMN III.
1. and Zu fled away and in his country concealed himself.
2. . . . . . opening his mouth like the venerable of heaven and earth
3. . . . . like mud
4. . . . . . was, the gods swept away
5. . . . . . I will not go he said.

6. To Nebo the powerful . . . . the child of Ishtar,

7. a speech he made to him also and spake to him:

8. Hero Nebo let there not be opposition in thee,

9. slay Zu with thy weapon.

10. May thy name be renowned in the assembly of the gods,

11. . . . . . made also fragrant with spices,

12. in the four regions they shall fix thy city.

13. May thy city be exalted like the temple,

14. they shall cry in the presence of the gods and praise thy name.

15. Nebo answered the speech,

16. to his father Anu word he spake:

17. Father to a desert country do thou consign him.

18. Let Zu not come among the gods thy sons,

1 9. for the *umsimi* he took in his hand,

20. the majesty he carried off he cast away the *parzi*,

21. and Zu fled away and in his country concealed himself.

22. . . . . . . opening his mouth like the venerable of heaven and earth

About ten lines lost here.

33. And thus the god . . . .

34. I also . . . .

35. and thus . . . .

36. He heard also . . . .

37. he turned . . . .

38. The god of noble face . . . .

39. to Anu . . . .

COLUMN IV. lost.

Such are the fragments of the story so far as they can be translated at present. The divine Zu here mentioned whose sin is spoken of is never counted among the gods, and there would be no clue to his nature were it not for a curious tablet printed in "Cuneiform Inscriptions," vol. iv. p. 14, from which it appears that he was in the likeness of a bird of prey. This tablet gives the following curious relation:

1. The god Sarturda (the lesser king) to a country a place remote [went],

2. in the land of Sabu . . . . . [he dwelt].

3. His mother had not placed him and had not . . . .

4. his father had not placed him and with him did not [go],

5. the strength of his knowledge . . . .

6. From the will of his heart a resolution he did not. . . .

7. In his own heart a resolution he made,

8. to the likeness of a bird he changed,

9. to the likeness of the divine storm bird (or Zu bird) he changed,

10. his wife forcibly he associated with,

11. the wife of the divine Zu bird, the son of the divine Zu bird,

12. in companionship he made sit.

13. The goddess Enna, the lady of Tigenna,

14. in the mountain he loved,

15. a female fashioned? of her mother in her likeness,

16. the goddess of perfumes a female fashioned? of her mother in her likeness

17. Her appearance was like bright ukni stone,

18. her girdle was adorned with silver and gold,

19. brightness was fixed in . . . .

20. brightness was set in . . . .

Many lines lost here, the story recommences on reverse.

1. . . . . . the crown he placed on his head

2. from the nest of the divine Zu bird he came.

This Zu bird I suppose to be the same as the god Zu of the inscriptions, his nature is shown by a passage in the annals of Assurnazirpal ("Cuneiform Inscriptions," vol. i. p. 22, col. ii. l. 107), where he says his warriors "like the divine zu bird upon them darted." This bird is called the cloud or storm bird, the flesh eating bird, the lion or giant bird, the bird of prey, the bird with sharp beak, and it evidently indicates some ravenous bird which was deified by the Babylonians. Some excellent remarks on the nature of this bird are given by Delitzsch in his "Assyrische studien," pp. 96, 116.

In the legend of Sarturda it is said that he changed into a Zu bird. Sarturda which may be explained "the young king" was lord of the city of Amarda or Marad, and he is said to have been the deity worshipped by Izdubar.

The Zu of the legend, who offends against Bel, I suppose to be the same as the divine bird of prey mentioned in the other inscriptions, otherwise we have no mention in any other inscription of this personage.

In the story of the offence of Zu there is another instance of the variations which constantly occur in the Assyrian inscriptions with respect to the relationship of the gods. Nebo is usually called son of Merodach, but in this inscription he is called son of Anu.

In my translation of the legend on K 3454, the sin of Zu is very obscure, and I am quite unable to see through the allusions in the text; but it is quite evident that his sin was considered to be great, as it raises the anger of Bel, and causes Anu to call on his sons in succession to slay Zu; while the sons of the god Anu request that he may be expelled from the company of the gods.

The second legend, in which the god Sarturda changes into a Zu bird, is as obscure as the first, there being also in this doubtful words and mutilated passages. Sarturda, although a celebrated god in early times, is seldom mentioned in the later inscriptions, and there is no information anywhere as to the females or goddesses mentioned in the legend. The idea of the gods sometimes changing themselves into animals was not uncommon in early times.

The explanation of these legends must be left until the meanings of several words in them are better known.

CHAPTER VIII: THE EXPLOITS OF LUBARA.

Lubara.—God of Pestilence.—Itak.—The Plague.—Seven warrior gods.—Destruction of people.—Anu.—Goddess of Karrak.—Speech of Elu.—Sin and destruction of Babylonians.—Shamas.—Sin and destruction of Erech.—Ishtar.—The great god and Duran.—Cutha.—Internal wars.—Itak goes to Syria.—Power and glory of Lubara.—Song of Lubara.—Blessings on his worship.—God Ner.—Prayer to arrest the Plague.

THE tablets recording this story (which I formerly called the "war of the gods") are five in number, but I have only discovered a few fragments of them. From the indications presented by these fragments I believe the first four tablets had each four columns of writing, and the fifth tablet was a smaller one of two columns to contain the remainder of the story.

The god whose exploits are principally recorded bears a name which I read with much hesitation as Lubara or Dabara and whom I conjecture on some doubtful grounds to be a form of the god Ninip.

The passages I have given in my "History of Assurbanipal" and in "Assyrian Discoveries," pp. 339, 340, 343, serve to show that this deity was the god of pestilence, or the personification of the plague, and the passage in the Deluge table ("Assyrian Discoveries," p. 192, l. 20), shows this name with the same meaning.

My reading Lubara is taken from the passage, "Cuneiform Inscriptions," vol. ii. p. 25, l. 13.

Lubara has a companion deity named Itak who marches before him, and seven gods who follow him in his destructive course.

The point of the story in these tablets appears to be, that the people of the world had offended Anu god of heaven, and that deity ordered Lubara to go forth and strike the people with the pest. It is evident here that exactly the same views prevailed in Babylonia as those among the Jews, visitations from pestilence or famine being always supposed to be sent by the deity in punishment for some sin.

The whole of this series of tablets may be described as a poetical picture of the destruction caused by a plague, sweeping over district after district, and destroying everything before it.

The fragment which appears to me to come first in the series is a very mutilated portion of a tablet, containing parts of three columns of writing. Only a fragment of the first column is perfect enough to translate, and the characters on this are so worn that the translation cannot be other than doubtful. It appears to read

1. to capture he was turned . . . .
2. the fifth time . . . . above and below seeking
3. seven I? say? strengthened . . . .
4. the words of the account of the seven gods all of them Anu heard and
5. he said? to them also to Lubara the warrior of the gods may thy hand move
6. like of the people of the nations their pit . . . . he will strike
7. set thy heart also to make a destruction
8. the people of the dark races to ruin thou shalt strike with the desolation of the god Ner
9. and thy weapon against their swords may thy hand move
10. slay them and cast down their weapons.
11. He said to Lubara do thou go and
12. thy . . . . like an old man, thy son name? afterwards?
13. like a slaughter in the house, name in the house,
14. against the seat devised . . . .
15. like in war not . . . .

This passage appears to describe the forthcoming
destruction, the god Anu commanding the slaughter. The next fragment is of a different character, but
appears from its style to belong to this series.

1. . . . . . he. . . .
2. . . . spake to him and he . . . .
3. . . . spake to him and he learned? . . .
4. Anu at the doing of Hea . .
5. the gods of heaven and earth all there were who thus answered
6. his will which was like the will of Anu who . . .
7. . . . . . extending from the horizon of heaven to the top of heaven
8. . . . . . looked and his fear he saw
9. . . . . . Anu who hand? over him . . . . made
10. . . . . of Hea his calamity made
11. . . . . . strong to later days to . . . .
12. . . . . . sin of mankind

13. . . . . . triumphantly the net . . he broke
14. . . . . . to heaven he ascended, she thus
15. . . . . . 4,021 people he placed
16. . . . . . the illness which was on the body of the people he placed
17. . . . . . the illness the goddess of Karrak made to cease

The next portion of the legend is a considerable part of one of the tablets, probably the fourth, all four columns of writing being represented. There are many curious points in this tablet, beside the special purpose of the legend, such as the peoples enumerated in the fourth column, the action of the gods of the various cities, &c.

COLUMN I.

1. . . . . . his . . thou dost not sweep away
2. . . . . . thou turnest his troop
3. . . . . dwelling
4. . . . . . thou enterest within it
5. . . . . . thou callest, like a tent
6. . . . . . an appointment has not
7. . . . . . thy . . . he gathers
8. . . . . . he draws out his sword
9. . . . . . he fills his bow
10. . . . . . war is made
11. . . . . . like a bird he flies
12. . . . . . and he seeks
13. . . . . . he destroys
14. . . . . . great curse
15. . . . . . strike their hands
16. . . . . . the fire
17. . . . . . taken
18. Elu his fierceness? covered? and
19. in his heart he said:
20. Lubara is couching at his gate, over the corpses of chiefs and slaves
21. thou placest his seat.
22. The wicked Babylonians watched it and
23. thou art their curse.
24. To the floor thou tramplest them and thou didst break through . . . .
25. Warrior Lubara.
26. Thou leavest also the land, thou goest out to another
27. . . . . . thou destroyest the land, thou enterest the palace.

28. The people see thee and they reach their weapons.

29. The high priest the avenger of Babylon hardens his heart,

30. like the spoiling of enemies to spoil he sends forth his soldiers.

31. Before the face of the people they do evil violently.

32. To that city I send thee, thou man

33. shalt not fear, do not tremble at a man.

34. Small and great at once cast down and

35. . . . . of evil leaving fear? thou dost not save any one.

36. The collection of the goods of Babylon thou spoilest,

37. the people the king gathers, and enters the city,

38. shaking the bow, raising the sword

39. of the people spoiled who are punished by Anu and Dagon.

40. Their swords thou takest,

41. their corpses like the pouring down of rain thou dost cast down in the vicinity of the city,

42. and their treasures thou openest, thou dost sweep into the river.

43. The great lord Merodach saw and angrily spoke,

44. in his heart he resolved,

45. on an unsparing curse his face is set,

46. . . . . of the river fled not . . . .

COLUMN II.

Many lines lost.

1. . . . . . of the lord of the earth . . . .

2. a deluge he did not make . . . .

3. Against Shamas his tower thou destroyest thou dost cast . . . .

4. Of Erech the seat of Anu and Ishtar

5. the city of the ladies, Samhati and Harimati,

6. of Ishtar. Death they fear they are delivered into thy hands.

7. The Suti with the Suti are placed in . . . .

8. slay the house of heaven, the priests, the festival makers,

9. who to make the people of Ishtar fear, their manhood turn to . . . .

10. carrying swords, carrying *naklabi*, *dupe*, and *zurri*

11. who to raise the spirit of Ishtar trust . . . .

12. the high priest, hardened, bows his face over them day and night?

13. Their foundations, their countenance turn . . . .

14. Ishtar is angry and troubled over the city of Erech,

15. the enemies she strikes and like corn on the waters she scatters.

16. Dwelling in his . . . . Parra . . . .

17. he does not lead the expedition?

18. The enemies whom thou destroyest do not return to . . . .

19. The great god answered the speech

20. The city of Duran to blood . . . .

21. the people who are in the midst of it like reeds are trembling

22. like sick? before the waters their pit . . . .

23. and of me thou dost not leave me

24. to the Suti . . . .

25. I in my city Duran judge uprightly

26. I do not . . . .

27. evil? I do not give and . . . .

28. the upright people I leave . . . .

29. a fire is fixed . . . .

Four other broken lines.

COLUMN III.

Many lines lost.

1. . . . . swear and the house . . . .

2. . . . . country and father . . . .

3. . . . . foundation and fixed . . . .

4. . . . . house built now . . . .

5. this all and the portion . . . .

6. the day he brought me fate I . . . .

7. him, his seat also he lays waste?

8. Afterwards may he waste to another . . . .

9. The warrior Lubara, the just also of Kutha?

10. and the unjust also of Kutha,

11. who sin against thee also in Kutha,

12. who do not sin against thee also in Kutha,

13. . . . . of the god of Kutha,

14. . . . . head of the king of Kutha?

Two other mutilated lines.

COLUMN IV.

1. The planet Jupiter fearing and . . . .

2. to his might . . . .

3. not rejoicing . . . .

4. who the side carried him, destroyed . . . .

5. to the seat of the king of the gods may he send and . . . .

6. The warrior Lubara heard also

7. the words Itak spoke to him then . . . .

8. and thus spake the warrior Lubara:

9. The sea coast with the sea coast, Subarta with Subarta, Assyrian with Assyrian.

10. Elamite with Elamite

11. Cossean with Cossean

12. Sutu with Sutu

13. Goim with Goim

14. Lulubu with Lulubu

15. Country with country, house with house, man with man,

16. brother with brother, in the country close together, and may they destroy each other,

17. and afterwards may the people of Akkad increase, and

18. the whole of them may they destroy, and fight against them.

19. The warrior Lubara to Itak who goes before him a word spake:

20. Go also Itak, in the word thou hast spoken do according to all thy heart.

21. Itak to the land of Syria set his face,

22. and the seven warrior gods unequalled

23. marched after him.

24. To the country of Syria the warrior went,

25. his hand he also lifted and destroyed the land,

26. the land of Syria he took for his country,

27. the forests of people . . . . he broke through the ranks?

28. . . . . like . . . .

The next fragments of the story are on a mutilated copy of the last tablet, K 1282. This tablet, as

I have before stated, is only a smaller supplemental one to include the end of the story, which could not be written on the fourth tablet.

K. 1282.

Obverse.

1. When Lubara . . . .

2. the gods all of them . . . .

3. the angels and spirits all . . . .

4. Lubara his mouth opened and . . . .

5. shake also the whole of you . . . .

6. I am placed? and in the first sin . . . .

7. my heart is angry and . . . .

8. like a flock of sheep may . . . .

9. against the setting up of boundaries . . . .

10. like spoiling the country right and . . . .

11. in the mouth of a dog noble?

12. and the place . . . .

Fifteen lines much broken here.

28. . . . . the land of Akkad its strength . . . .

29. one of thy seven chiefs like . . . .

30. his cities to ruins and mounds thou dost reduce . . . .

31. his great spoil thou dost spoil, to the midst of. . . .

32. the gods of the country strong thou removest afar off . . . .

33. the god Ner and . . . .

34. the productions of the countries . . . .

35. within it they gather . . . .

Four mutilated lines here.

Reverse.

1. For years untold the glory of the great lord. . . .

2. When Lubara was angry also to sweep the countries . . . .

3. he set . . . . his face

4. Itak his adviser quieted him and stayed . . . .

6. collecting his . . . . to the mighty one of the gods, Merodach son of . . .

7. in the commencement of the . night he sent him, and like in the year . .

8. Not any one . . . .

9. . . . . and went not down against . . . .

10. his . . . . also Lubara received and before . . . .

11. . . . . Itak went before him rejoicing . . . .

12. . . . . all of them placed with him.

13. Any one who shall speak of the warrior Lubara

14. and that song shall glorify; in his place, thou wilt guard continually . .

15. . . . . cover and may he not fall? . . . . .

16. his name shall be proclaimed over the world.

17. Whoever my heroism shall recount,

18. an adversary may he not meet.

19. The prophet who shall cry it out, shall not die by the chastisement;

20. higher than king and prince he shall raise his people.

21. The tablet writer who studies it and flees from the wicked, shall be great in the land.

22. In the places of the people the established places, my name they proclaim,

23. their ears I open.

24. In the house the place where their goods are placed, when Lubara is angry

25. may the seven gods turn him aside,

26. may the chastising sword not touch him whose face thou establishest.

27. That song for ever may they establish and may they fix the part . . . .

28. the countries all of them may they hear, and glorify my heroism;

29. the people of all the cities may they see, and exalt my name.

Fifth tablet of the exploits of . . . .

Here we see a picture of Oriental feeling with reference to natural phenomenon or disaster to mankind. It is supposed that some deity or angel stands with a sword over the devoted people and sweeps them into eternity.

What these Babylonians had been guilty of the record is not perfect enough to show. The first fragment shows the anger of Anu at their sin or supposed sin and his command to Lubara to take his weapon, slay the people, and desolate the land like the God Ner. This god Ner was a legendary being believed in at the time of Izdubar, who is mentioned as having a terrible name and being with Etana a dweller in Hades.

The next fragment exhibits the goddess of Karrak as healing the illness of some of the people, 4102 being mentioned as struck with disease.

In the next and largest fragment the story becomes a little more connected, it commences with a description of preparation for battle, and goes on through speeches and actions to describe the course of Lubara and his plague over Babylon, where he spares neither chief nor slave, and enters even the palace. It is supposed in lines 29–31 that the sin of the Babylonians arose from the chief priest or governor of the city arming the troops and sending them out to plunder the people. For this the plague is sent, and its progress is graphically described. The next city visited belongs to Shamas, being either Larsa, or Sippara, and then the plague reaches Erech. The character of this city is described, the Venus worship, the women of pleasure Samhati and Harimati, the priests and ceremonies, and the progress of the plague over the place. Then the great god the deity of

Duran comes forward and pleads for his city, calling to mind its uprightness and justice, and praying its exemption from the plague.

Cutha is next mentioned in the obscure third column, and then the fourth column describes a prophecy of Lubara that there should be internal war among the Mesopotamian peoples of the sea-coast, Subarti, Assyrians, Elamites, Cosseans, Guti, Goim, and Lulubu, from all which troubles benefit should come to the Akkadians or upper Babylonians.

Then according to his wish Lubara sends Itak his servant, with the seven warrior gods to destroy Syria, and Itak sweeps over the country and destroys it.

The last tablet deals in generalities pointing out the action of Lubara when his praise was neglected, and telling all the glories and good that should come to those who should spread a song in honour of this deity. On the spread of a plague it is evident that the Babylonians had no better means of arresting it than to pray and praise the supposed terrible deity of the scourge, that he might sheathe his sword of anger.

CHAPTER IX: BABYLONIAN FABLES.

Fables.—Common in the East.—Description.—Power of speech in animals.—Story of the eagle.—Serpent.—Shamas.—The eagle caught.—Eats the serpent.—Anger of birds.—Etana.—Seven gods.—Third tablet.—Speech of eagle.—Story of the fox.—His cunning.—Judgment of Shamas.—His show of sorrow.—His punishment.—Speech of fox:—Fable of the horse and ox.—They consort together.—Speech of the ox.—His good fortune.—Contrast with the horse.—Hunting the ox.—Speech of the horse.—Offers to recount story.—Story of Ishtar.—Further tablets.

COMBINED with these stories of the gods, traditions of the early history of man, and accounts of the Creation, are fragments of a series in which the various animals speak and act. I call these tablets "Fables" to distinguish them from the others, but, as many of the others are equally fabulous and very similar in style, the name must not be taken to imply any distinctive character in this direction. It is probable that all these stories even in Babylonia were equally believed in by the devout and the ignorant, treated as allegories by the poets, and repudiated as fabulous by the learned. In the "Fables" or stories in which animals play prominent parts, each creature is endowed with the power of speech, and this idea was common even in that day in the whole of Western Asia and Egypt, it is found in various Egyptian stories, it occurs in Genesis, where we have a speaking serpent, in Numbers where Balaam's ass reproves his master, and in the stories of Jotham and Joash, where the trees are made to speak; again in the Izdubar legends, where the trees answer Heabani.

These legends so far as I have discovered are four in number.

The first contained at least four tablets each having four columns of writing. Two of the acting animals in it are the eagle and the serpent.

The second is similar in character, the leading animal being the fox or jackal, there are only four fragments, and I have no evidence as to the number of tablets; this may belong to the same series as the fable of the eagle.

The third is a single tablet with two columns of writing, it is a discussion between the horse and ox.

The fourth is a single fragment in which a calf speaks, but there is nothing to show the nature of the story.

I. THE STORY OF THE EAGLE.

This story appears to be the longest and most curious of these legends, but the very mutilated condition of the various fragments gives as usual considerable difficulty in attempting an explanation. One of the actors in the story is an ancient monarch named Etana who is mentioned as already dead, and as being an inhabitant of the infernal regions in the time of Izdubar.

I am unable to ascertain the order of the fragments of these legends and must translate them as they come.

K 2527.

Many lines lost at commencement.

1. The serpent in . . .
2. I give command? . . . . . .
3. to the eagle . . . . . .
4. Again the nest . . . . . .
5. my nest I leave . . . . . .
6. the assembly? of my people . . . . . .
7. I go down and enter?
8. the sentence which Shamas has pronounced on me . . . . . .
9. I feel? Shamas thy sight? in the earth . . . .
10. thy stroke? this . . . .
11. in thy sight? let me not . . . .
12. doing evil the goddess Bau (Gula) was . . . .
13. The sorrow of the serpent [shamas saw and]
14. Shamas opened his mouth and word he spoke to. . . .
15. Go the way . . . . pass . . . .
16. I cut thee off? . . . .
17. open also his heart . . . .
18. . . . . he placed . . . .
19. . . . . birds of heaven . . .

Reverse.

1. The eagle with them . . . .
2. the god? knew . . . .
3. to enter to the food he sought . . . .
4. to cover the . . . .
5. to the midst at his entering . . . .

6. enclosed the feathers of his wings . . . .

7. his claws? and his pinions to . . . .

8. dying of hunger and thirst . . . .

9. at the work of Shamas the warrior, the serpent. . . .

10. he took also the serpent to . . . .

11. he opened also his heart . . . .

12. seat he placed . . .

13. the anger of the birds of heaven . . . .

14. May the eagle . . . .

15. with the young of the birds . . . .

16. The eagle opened his mouth . . . .

Five other mutilated lines.

On another fragment are the following few words:—

Obverse.

1. . . . issu to him also . . . .

2. . . . god my father . . . .

3. like Etana kill thee . . . .

4. like me . . . .

5. Etana the king . . . .

6. took him . . . .

Reverse.

1. Within the gate of Anu, Elu . . . .

2. . . . . .we will fix . . . .

3. within the gate of sin, Shamas, Vul and . . . .

4. . . . . . I opened . . . .

5. . . . . . I sweep . . . .

6. . . . . in the midst . . . .

7. the king . . . .

8. turned? and . . . .

9. I cover the throne . . . .

10. I take also . . . .

11. and greatly I break . . . .

12. The eagle to him also to Etana . . . .

13. I fear the serpent?

14. the course do thou fix for me . . . .

15. . . . . make me great . . . .

The next fragment, K 2606, is curious, as containing an account of some early legendary story in Babylonian history. This tablet formed the third in the series, and from it we gain part of the title of the tablets.

K 2606.

1. . . . . placed . . . .
2. . . . back bone . . . .
3. this . . . . placed . . .
4. . . . . fixed its brickwork . . . .
5. . . . . to the government of them . . . .
6. Etana he gave them . . . .
7. . . . . sword . . . .
8. the seven spirits . . . .
9. . . . . they took their counsel . . . .
10. . . . . placed in the country . . . .
11. . . . . all of them the angels . . . .
12. . . . . they . . . .
13. In those days also . . . .
14. and a sceptre of ukni stone . . . .
15. to rule the country . . . .
16. the seven gods over the people they raised . . . .
17. over the cities they raised . . . .
18. the city of the angels Surippak?
19. Ishtar to the neighbourhood to . . . .
20. and the king flew . . . .
21. Inninna to the neighbourhood . . . .
22. and the king flew . . . .
23. Elu encircled the sanctuary of . . . .
24. he sought also . . . .
25. in the wide country . . . .
26. the kingdom . . . .
27. he took and
28. the gods of the country
Reverse.
Many lines lost.
1. from of old he caused to wait . . . .

2.. Third tablet of "The city they . . . .

---

3. The eagle his mouth opened and to Shamas his lord he spake

The next fragment is a small portion probably of the fourth tablet.

1. The eagle his mouth opened . . . .

2. . . . .

3. the people of the birds . . . .

4. . . . .

5. angrily he spake . . . .

6. angrily I speak . . . .

7. in the mouth of Shamas the warrior . . . .

8. the people of the birds . . . .

9. The eagle his mouth opened and . . . .

10. Why comest thou . . . .

11. Etana his mouth opened and . . . .

12. speech? . . . . he . . . .

Such are the principal fragments of this curious legend. According to the fragment K 2527, the serpent had committed some sin for which it was condemned by the god Shamas to be eaten by the eagle; but the eagle declined the repast.

After this, some one, whose name is lost, baits a trap for the eagle, and the bird going to get the meat, falls into the trap and is caught. Now the eagle is left, until dying for want of food it is glad to eat the serpent, which it takes and tares open. The other birds then take offence, and desire that the eagle should be excluded from their ranks.

The other fragments concern the building of some city, Etana being king, and in these relations the eagle again appears, there are seven spirits or angels principal actors in the matter, but the whole story is obscure at present, and a connected plot cannot be made out.

This fable has evidently some direct connection with the mythical history of Babylonia, for Etana is mentioned as an ancient Babylonian monarch in the Izdubar legends. His memory was cherished as belonging to one of the terrible monarchs who were inhabiting Hades, probably on account of their deeds.

II. STORY OF THE FOX.

The next fable, that of the fox, is perhaps part of the same story, the fragments are so disconnected that they must be given without any attempt at arrangement.

K. 3641.

COLUMN I.

1. To. . . .

2. the people . . . .

3. father . . . .

4. mother called . . . .

5. he had asked and . . . .

6. he had raised life . . . .

7. thou in that day also . . . .

8. thou knowest enticing? and cunning, thou . . . .

9. of . . . . chains, his will he . . . .

10. about the rising of the jackal also he sent me let not . . . .

11. in a firm command he set my feet,

12. again by his will is the destruction of life.

13. Shamas in thy sentence, the answer? let him not escape,

14. by wisdom and cunning let them put to death the fox.

---

15. The fox on hearing this, bowed his head in the presence of Shamas and wept.

16. To the powerful presence of Shamas he went in his tears:

17. With this sentence O Shamas do not destroy me,

(Columns II. and III. lost.)

COLUMN IV.

1. Go to my forest, do not turn back afterwards

2. . . . . shall not come out, and the sun shall not be seen,

3. thou, any one shall not cut thee off . . . .

4. by the anger of my heart and fierceness of my face thou shalt fear before me,

5. may they keep thee and I will not . . . .

6. may they take hold of thee and not . . . .

7. may they bind thee and not . . . .

8. may they fell thy limbs . . . .

9. Then wept the jackal . . . .

10. he bowed his head . . . .

11. thou hast fixed . . . .

12. taking the . . . .

Four other mutilated lines.

The next fragment has lost the commencements and ends of all the lines.

1. . . . . . carried in his mouth . . . .

2. . . . . . before his . . . .

3. . . . . thou knowest wisdom and all . .

4. . . . . in . . . . of the jackal it was . . . .

5. . . . . in the field the fox . . . .

6. . . . . was decided under the ruler the . . . .

7. . . . . all laying down under him and of . . . .

8. . . . . he . . . . also . . . . he fled . . . .

9 . . . . . angry command, and not any one . . . .

10. . . . . mayest thou become old . . . . and take. . . .

11. . . . . in those days also the fox carried . . . .

12. . . . . the people he spoke. Why . . . .

13. . . . . the dog is removed and . . . .

The following fragment is in similar condition.

1. . . . . The limbs not . . . .

2. . . . . I did not weave and unclothed I am not. . . .

3. . . . . stranger I know . . . .

4. . . . . I caught and I surrounded . . . .

5. . . . from of old also the dog was my brother . . .

6. . . . . he begot me, a good place . .

7. . . . . of the city of Nisin I of Bel . . . .

8. . . . . limbs and the bodies did not stand . . .

9. . . . . life I did not end . . . .

10. . . . . brought up . . . . me . . . .

The fourth fragment contains only five legible lines.

1. . . . . was placed also right and left . .

2. . . . . their ruler sought . . . . .

3. . . . . let it not be . . . .

4. . . . he feared and did not throw down his spoil . . .

---

5. . . . fox in the forest . . . .

The last fragment is a small scrap, at the end of which the fox petitions Shamas to spare him.

The incidental allusions in these fragments show that the fox or jackal was even then considered cunning, and the animal in the story was evidently a watery specimen, as he brings tears to his assistance whenever anything is to be gained by it. He had offended Shamas by some means and the god sentenced him to death, a sentence which he escaped through powerful pleading on his own behalf.

III. FABLE OF THE HORSE AND OX.

The next fable, that of the horse and the ox, is a single tablet with only two columns of text. The date of the tablet is in the reign of Assurbanipal, and there is no statement that it is copied from an earlier text. There are altogether four portions of the text, but only one is perfect enough to be worth translating. This largest fragment, K 3456, contains about one third of the story.

K 3456.

(Several lines lost at commencement.)

1. . . . . the river . . . .
2. of food . . . . rest . . . .
3. height . . . . the Tigris situated
4. they ended . . . . was . . . .
5. in the flowers . . . . they disported in the floods?
6. the high places . . . . appearance
7. the vallies . . . . the country
8. at the appearance . . . . made the timid afraid
9. a boundless place . . . . he turned
10. in the side . . . .
11. of the waste . . . . earth were free within it
12. the tribes of beasts rejoiced in companionship and friendship,
13. between the ox and the horse friendship was made,
14. they rejoiced their . . . . over the friendship,
15. they consorted and pleased their hearts, and were prosperous.
16. The ox opened his mouth, and spake and said to the horse glorious in war:
17. I am pondering now upon the good fortune at my hand.
18. From the beginning of the year to the end of the year I ponder at my appearance.
19. He destroyed abundance of food, he dried up rivers of waters,
20. in the flowers he rolled, a carpet he made,
21. the vallies and springs he made for his country,
22. the high places he despised, he raged in the floods,
23. the sight of his horns make the timid afraid,
24. A boundless place is portioned for his . . . .
25. the man . . . . learned ceased . . . .
26. he broke the ropes and waited . . . .
27. and the horse will not approach a child, and he drives him . . . .
28. they catch thee thyself

29. he ascends also . . . .

Here the ox gives a good picture of his state and enjoyment, and looks with contempt on the horse because he is tamed.

After this comes a speech from the horse to the bull, the rest of the tablet being occupied by speeches and answers between the two animals. Most of these speeches are lost or only present in small fragments, and the story recommences on the reverse with the end of a speech from the horse.

1. fate . . . .
2. strong brass? . . . .
3. like with a cloak I am clothed and . . . .
4. over me any one not suited . . . .
5. king, high priest, lord and prince do not seek . . . .

---

6. The ox opened his mouth and spake and said to the horse glorious . . . .
7. I say I am noble and thou gatherest . . . .
8. in thy fighting why . . . .
9. the lord of the chariot destroys me and desolation . . . .
10. in my body I am firm . . . .
11. in my inside I am firm . . . .
12. the warrior draws out of his quiver . . . .
13. strength carries a curse . . . .
14. the weapon of my masters over . . . .
15. he causes to see servitude like . . . .
16. . . . . in thee is not . . . .
17. he causes to go on the path over . . . .

---

18. The horse opened his mouth and spake arid said to the ox . . . .
19. In my hearing . . . .
20. the weapon . . . .
21. the swords . . . .
22. . . . . . .
23. strength? of the heart which does not . . . .
24. in crossing that river . . . .
25. in the paths of thy country . . . .
26. I reveal? ox the story . . . .
27. in thy appearance, it is not . . . .
28. thy splendour is subdued? . . . .

29. like . . . . the horse . . . .

---

30. The ox opened his mouth and spake and said to the horse . . . .

31. Of the stories which thou tellest . . . .

32. open first (that of) "When the noble Ishtar. . . .

(Colophon)

Palace of Assurbanipal, king of nations, king . . .

It appears from these fragments that the story described a time when the animals associated together, and the ox and horse fell into a friendly conversation. The ox, commencing the discussion, praised himself; the answer of the horse is lost, but where the story recommences it appears that the ox objects to the horse drawing the chariot from which he (the ox) is hunted, and the horse ultimately offers to tell the ox a story, the ox choosing the story called "When the noble Ishtar ", probably some story of the same character as Ishtar's descent into Hades.

It is uncertain if any other tablet followed this; it is, however, probable that there was one containing the story told by the horse. Although there is no indication to show the date of this fable, I should think, by the style and matter, it belonged to about the same date as the other writings given in this volume. The loss of the tablet containing the story of Ishtar, told by the horse to the ox, is unfortunate. It is evident that Ishtar was a very celebrated goddess, and her adventures formed the subject of many narratives. Some of the words and forms in these fables are exactly the same as those used in the Izdubar and Creation legends, and in all these stories the deity Shamas figures more prominently than is usual in the mythology. The last fable is a mere fragment similar to the others, containing a story in which the calf speaks. There is not enough of this to make it worth translation.

CHAPTER X: FRAGMENTS OF MISCELLANEOUS TEXTS.

Atarpi.—Sin of the world.—Mother and daughter quarrel.—Zamu.—Punishment of world.—Hea.—Calls his sons.—Orders drought.—Famine.—Building.—Nusku.—Riddle of wise man.—Nature and universal presence of air.—Gods.—Sinuri.—Divining by fracture of reed.—Incantation.—Dream.—Tower of Babel.—Obscurity of legend.—Not noticed by Berosus.—Fragmentary tablet.—Destruction of Tower.—Dispersion.—Locality Babylon.—Birs Nimrud.—Babil.—Assyrian representations.

I HAVE included in this chapter a number of stories of a similar character to those of Genesis, but which are not directly connected, and a fragment relating to the tower of Babel. The first and principal text is the story of Atarpi, or Atarpi-nisi. 'This story is on a tablet in six columns, and there is only one copy. It is very mutilated, very little being preserved except Column III., and there are numerous repetitions throughout the text. The inscription has originally been a long one, probably extending to about 400 lines of writing, the text differs from the generality of these inscriptions, being very obscure and difficult. In consequence of this and other reasons, I only give an outline of most of the story.

We are first told of a quarrel between a mother and her daughter, and that the mother shuts the door of the house, and turns her daughter adrift. The doings of a man named Zamu have some connection with the affair; and at the close we are told of Atarpi, sometimes called Atarpi-nisi, or Atarpi the "man" who had his couch beside a river, and was pious to the gods, but took no notice of these things. Where the story next opens, the god Elu or Bel calls together an assembly of the gods his sons, and relates to them that he is angry at the sin of the world, stating also that he will bring down upon them disease, poison, and distress. This is followed by the statement that these things came to pass, and Atarpi then invoked the god Hea to remove these evils. Hea answers, and announces his resolve to destroy the people. After this the story reads:

1. Hea called his assembly he said to the gods his sons

2. . . . . I made them

3. . . . shall not stretch until before he turns.

4. Their wickedness I am angry at,

5. their punishment shall not be small,

6. I will look to judge the people,

7. in their stomach let food be exhausted,

8. above let Vul drink up his rain,

9. let the lower regions be shut up, and the floods not be carried in the streams,

10. let the ground be hardened which was overflown,

11. let the growth of corn cease, may blackness overspread the fields,

12. let the plowed fields bring forth thorns,

13. may the cultivation be broken up, food not arise and it not produce,

14. may distress be spread over the people,

15. may favour be broken off, and good not be given.

---

16. He looked also to judge the people,

17. in their stomach food he exhausted,

18. Above Vul drank up his rains,

19. the lower regions were shut up, and floods not carried in the streams,

20. The ground was hardened which had been overflown,

21. the growth of corn ceased, blackness spread over the fields,

22. the plowed fields brought forth thorns, the cultivation was broken up,

23. food did not rise, and it did not produce,

24. distress was spread over the people,

25. favour was broken off, good was not given.

This will serve to show the style of the tablet. The instrument of punishment was apparently a famine from want of rain, but there are some obscure words even in this passage.

Here the story is again lost, and where it recommences some one is making a speech, directing another person to cut something into portions, and place seven on each side, then to build brickwork round them. After this comes a single fragment, the connection of which with the former part is obscure.

1. I curse the goddess . . . .

2. to her face also . . . .

---

3. Anu opened his mouth and spake and said to Nusku

4. Nusku open thy gate thy weapons take

5. in the assembly of the great gods the will?

6. their speech?

7. Anu has sent me . . . .

8. your king has sent?

At present no satisfactory story can be made out of the detached fragments of this tablet, but it evidently belongs to the mythical portion of Babylonian history.

The next text is a single fragment, K 2407, belonging to a curious story of a wise man who puts a riddle to the gods.

K 2407.

(Many lines lost.)

1. which in the house is . . . .

2. which in the secret place is . . . .

3. which is in the foundation of the house . . . .

4. which on the floor? of the house stands, which. . . .

5. which in the vicinity . . . .

6. which by the sides of the house goes down . . . .

7. which in the ditch of the house open, lays down. . . .

8. which roars like a bull, which brays like an ass,

9. which flutters like a sail, which bleats like a sheep,

10. which barks like a dog,

11. which growls like a bear,

12. which into the breast of a man enters, which into the breast of a woman enters.

13. Sar-nerra heard the word which the wise son of man

14. asked, and all the gods he sent to:

15. Friends are ye I am unable? . . . . to you

After this there is a mutilated passage containing the names, titles, and actions of the gods who consider the riddle. It is evident that it is air or wind which the wise man means in his riddle, for this is everywhere, and in its sounds imitates the cries of animals.

Next we have another single fragment about a person named Sinuri, who uses a divining rod to ascertain the meaning of a dream.

1. Sinuri with the cut reed pondered . . . .

2. with his right hand he broke it, and Sinuri spake and thus said:

p. 158

3. Now the plant of Nusku, shrub? of Shamas at thou,

96

4. Judge, thou judgest (or divinest), divine concerning this dream,

5. which in the evening, at midnight, or in the morning,

6. has come, which thou knowest, but I do not know.

7. If it be good may its good not be lost to me,

8. if it be evil may its evil not happen to me.

There are some more obscure and broken lines, but

no indication as to the story to which it belongs.

One of the most obscure incidents in the Book of Genesis is undoubtedly the building of the Tower of Babel. So far as we can judge from the fragments of his copyists, there was no reference to it in the work of Berosus, and early writers had to quote from writers of more than doubtful authority in order to confirm it.

There is also no representation on any of the Babylonian gems which can with any certainty be described as belonging to this story. I have, however, picked out three from a series of these carvings which I think may be distorted representations of the event. In these and some others of the same sort, figures have their hands on tall piles, as if erecting them; and there is a god always represented near, in much the same attitude. There is no proper proportion between the supposed structure and the men, and I would not urge more than a possible connection with the myth. The utter absence of any allusion to the tower, either in Berosus or the inscriptions, led me to doubt at one time if the story. ever formed part of the Babylonian history.

Early this year I was astonished to find, on having one of the Assyrian fragments cleaned, that it contained a mutilated account of part of the story of the tower. I have since searched through the whole collection, but have been unable to find any more of this tablet, except two minute fragments which add nothing to the text.

It is evident from the wording of the fragment that it was preceded by at least one tablet, describing the sin of the people in building the tower. The fragment preserved belongs to a tablet containing from four to six columns of writing, of which fragments of four remain. The principal part is the beginning of Column I.

COLUMN I.

1. . . . . . them? the father . . . .

2. . . . . . of him, his heart was evil,

3. . . . . . against the father of all the gods was wicked,

4. . . . . of him, his heart was evil,

5. . . . . . Babylon brought to subjection,

6. [small] and great he confounded their speech.

7. . . . . Babylon brought to subjection,

8. [small] and great he confounded their speech.

9. their strong place (tower) all the day they founded;

10. to their strong place in the night

11. entirely he made an end.

12. In his anger also word thus he poured out:

13. [to] scatter abroad he set his face

14. he gave this? command, their counsel was confused

15. . . . . . the course he broke

16. . . . . . fixed the sanctuary

There is a small fragment of Column II., but the connection with Column I. is not apparent.

COLUMN II.

1. Sar-tul-elli . . . .

2. in front carried Anu . . . .

3. to Bel-sara his father . . . .

4. like his heart also . . . .

5. which carried wisdom . . . .

6. In those days also . . . .

7. he carried him . . . .

8. Nin-kina . . . .

9. My son I rise and . . . .

10. his number(?) . . . .

11. entirely . . . .

There is a third portion on the same tablet belonging to a column on the other side, either the third or the fifth.

REVERSE COLUMN III. OR V.

1. In . . . .

2. he blew and . . . .

3. for a long time in the cities . . . .

4. Nunanner went . . . .

5. He said, like heaven and earth . . .

p. 162

6. that path they went . . . .

7. fiercely they approached to the presence . . . .

8. he saw them and the earth . . . .

9. of stopping not . . . .

10. of the gods . . . .

11. the gods looked . . . .

12. violence(?) . . . .

13. Bitterly they wept at Babi . . . .

14. very much they grieved . . . .

15. at their misfortune and . . . .

These fragments are so remarkable that it is most unfortunate we have not the remainder of the tablet.

In the first part we have the anger of the gods at the sin of the world, the place mentioned being Babylon. The building or work is called tazimat or tazimtu, a word meaning strong, and there is a curious relation, lines 9 to 11, that what they built in the day the god destroyed in the night.

The remainder of the fragment and the two fragments of the other columns agree with the story as far as their mutilated condition allows. The fractured end of the 13th line of the third fragment has the beginning of a name Babi, which may be completed Babil or Babel, but I have not ventured on the restoration. In the case of the 6th and 8th lines of the first fragment I have translated the word "speech" with a prejudice; I have never seen the Assyrian word with this meaning.

The whole account is at present so fragmentary that I think it better to make no detailed comparisons until more of the text is obtained. The various notices which have come down to us seem to me to point to the great pile of Birs Nimrud, near Babylon, as the site of the tower, this opinion is held by Sir Henry Rawlinson and most other authorities of weight. This ruin has been examined by Sir Henry Rawlinson; details of his operations here are given in "Jour. Asiatic Soc.," vol. xviii., and Rawlinson's "Ancient Monarchies," p. 544. Sir Henry discovered by excavation that the tower consisted of seven stages of brickwork on an earthen platform, each stage being of a different colour. The temple was devoted to the seven planets; the height of the earthen platform was not ascertained, the first stage, which was an exact square, was 272 feet each way, and 26 feet high, the bricks blackened with bitumen; this stage is supposed to have been devoted to the planet Saturn. The second stage was a square of 230 feet, 26 feet high, faced with orange-coloured bricks; supposed to be devoted to Jupiter. The third stage, 188 feet square, and 26 feet high, faced with red bricks, was probably dedicated to Mars. The fourth stage, 146 feet square, and 15 feet high, was probably devoted to the Sun, and is supposed by Sir H. Rawlinson to have been originally plated with gold. The fifth stage is supposed to have been 104, the sixth 62, and the seventh 20 feet square, but the top was too ruinous to decide these measurements. These stages were probably devoted to Venus, Mercury, and the Moon. Each stage of the building was not set in the centre of the stage on which it rested, but was placed 30 feet from the front, and 12 feet from the back. The ruin at present rises 154 feet above the level of the plain, and is the most imposing pile in the whole country. The only other ruin which has any claim to represent the tower is the Babil mound within the enclosure of Babylon, which is the site of the Temple of Bel. I have given views of both ruins as the possible alternative sites.

In the Babylonian and Assyrian sculptures there are occasionally representations of towers similar in style to the supposed Tower of Babel; one of these is given on the stone of Merodach Baladan I., opposite p. 236 of "Assyrian Discoveries;" another occurs on the sculptures at Nineveh, representing the city of Babylon; this tower is probably the Borsippa pile, which is supposed to represent the Tower of Babel. Birs Nimrud now consists of seven stages, but the top stages were only built by Nebuchadnezzar; before his time it probably presented the appearance shown in the Assyrian sculpture, and in the similar Babylonian representation figured opposite page 236 of "Assyrian Discoveries."

CHAPTER XI: THE IZDUBAR LEGENDS.

Account of Deluge.—Nimrod.—Izdubar.—Age of Legends.—
Babylonian cylinders.—Notices of Izdubar.—Surippak.—Ark City.—
Twelve tablets.—Extent of Legends.—Description.—Introduction.—
Meeting of Heabani and Izdubar.—Destruction of tyrant Humbaba.—
Adventures of Ishtar.—Illness and wanderings of Izdubar.—
Description of Deluge and conclusion.—First Tablet.—Kingdom of
Nimrod.—Traditions.—Identifications.—Translation.—Elamite
Conquest.—Dates.

THESE legends, which I discovered in 1872, are principally of interest from their containing the Chaldean account of the Deluge. I have published the most perfect portions in various forms since, the most complete account being in my "Assyrian Discoveries." These legends have also been commented upon by M. Lenormant in his "Les Premières Civilizations," and by Mr. Fox Talbot in the "Transactions of the Society of Biblical Archæology."

The Izdubar legends give, I believe, the history of the Biblical hero Nimrod. They record the adventures of a famous sovereign of Babylonia whom I provisionally call Izdubar, but whose name cannot at present be phonetically rendered. He appears to me to be the monarch who bears the closest resemblance in his fame and actions to the Nimrod of the Bible.

Since the first discovery of his history, very little light has been thrown on the age and exploits of Izdubar. Among all the references and allusions there is nothing exact or satisfactory to fix his place in the scheme of Babylonian history. The age of the legends of Izdubar in their present form is unknown, but may fairly be placed about B.C. 2000. As these stories were traditions in the country before they were committed to writing, their antiquity as traditions is probably much greater than that.

The earliest evidence we have of these traditions is in the carvings on early Babylonian cylindrical seals. Among the earliest known devices on these seals we have scenes from the legends of Izdubar, and from the story of the Creation. These seals belong to the age of the kings of Akkad and of Ur, and some of them may be older than B.C. 2000. The principal incidents represented on these seals are the struggles of Izdubar and his companion

Heabani with the lion and the bull, the journey of Izdubar ih search of Hasisadra, Noah or Hasisadra in his ark, and the war between Tiamat the sea-dragon and the god Merodach. There is a fragment of one document in the British Museum which claims to be copied from an omen tablet belonging to the time of Izdubar himself, but it is probably not earlier than B.C. 1600, when many similar tablets were written. There is an incidental notice of Izdubar and his ship, in allusion to the story of his wanderings, in the tablet printed in "Cuneiform Inscriptions," vol. ii. p. 46. This tablet, which contains lists of wooden objects, was written in the time of Assurbanipal, but is copied from an original, which must have been written at least eighteen hundred years before the Christian era. The geographical notices on this tablet suit the period between B.C. 2000 and 1800, long before the rise of Babylon. In this tablet Surippak is called the ship or ark city, this name forming another reference to the Flood legends. Izdubar is also mentioned in a series of tablets relating to witchcraft, and on a tablet containing prayers to him as a god; this last showing that he was deified, an honour also given to several other Babylonian kings.

The legends of Izdubar are inscribed on twelve tablets, of which there are remains of at least four editions. Ail the tablets are in fragments, and none of them are complete; but it is a fortunate circumstance that the most perfect tablet is the eleventh, which describes the Deluge, this being the most important of the series. In chapter i. I have described the successive steps in the discovery of these legends, and may now pass on to the description and translation of the various fragments. All the fragments of our present copies belong, as I have before stated, to the reign of Assurbanipal, king of Assyria, in the seventh century B.C. From the mutilated condition of many of them it is impossible at present to gain an accurate idea of the whole scope of the legends, and many parts which are lost have to be supplied by conjecture, the order even of some of the tablets cannot be determined, and it is uncertain if we have fragments of the whole twelve tablets; in my present account, however, I have conjecturally divided the fragments into groups corresponding roughly with the subjects of the tablets. Each tablet when complete contained six columns of writing, and each column had generally from forty to fifty lines of writing, there being in all about 3,000 lines of cuneiform text. The divisions I have adopted will be seen by the following summary, which exhibits my present knowledge of the fragments.

Part I.—Introduction.

Tablet I.—Number of lines uncertain, probably about 240. First column initial line preserved, second column lost, third column twenty-six lines preserved, fourth column doubtful fragment inserted, fifth and sixth columns lost.

Probable subjects: conquest of Babylonia by the Elamites, birth and parentage of Izdubar.

Part II.—Meeting of Heabani and Izdubar.

Tablet II.—Number of lines uncertain, probably about 240. First and second columns lost, third and fourth columns about half preserved, fifth and sixth columns lost.

Tablet III.—Number of lines about 270. First column fourteen lines preserved, second, third, fourth and fifth columns nearly perfect, sixth column a fragment.

Probable subjects: dream of Izdubar, Heabani invited comes to Erech, and explains the dream.

Part III.—Destruction of the tyrant Humbaba.

Tablet IV.—Number of lines probably about 260. About one-third of first, second, and third columns, doubtful fragments of fourth, fifth, and sixth columns.

Tablet V.—Number of lines about 260. Most of first column, and part of second column preserved, third, fourth, and fifth columns lost, fragment of sixth column.

Probable subjects: contests with wild animals, Izdubar and Heabani slay the tyrant Humbaba.

Part IV.—Adventures of Ishtar.

Tablet VI.—Number of lines about 210. Most of first column preserved, second column nearly perfect, third and fourth columns partly preserved, fifth and sixth columns nearly perfect.

Tablet VII.—Number of lines probably about 240. First line of first column preserved, second column lost, third and fourth column partly preserved, fifth and sixth columns conjecturally restored from tablet of descent of Ishtar into Hades.

Probable subjects: Ishtar loves Izdubar, her amours, her ascent to heaven, destruction of her bull, her descent to hell.

Part V.—Illness and wanderings of Izdubar.

Tablet VIII.—Number of lines probably about 270. Conjectured fragments of first, second, and third columns, fourth and fifth columns lost, conjectured fragments of sixth column.

Tablet IX.—Number of lines about 190. Portions of all six columns preserved.

Tablet X.—Number of lines about 270. Portions of all six columns preserved.

Probable subjects: discourse to trees, dreams, illness of Izdubar, death of Heabani, wanderings of Izdubar in search of the hero of the Deluge.

Part VI—Description of Deluge, and conclusion.

Tablet XI.—Number of lines 294. All six columns nearly perfect.

Tablet XII.—Number of lines about 200. Portions of first four columns preserved, two lines of fifth column, sixth column perfect.

Probable subjects: description of Deluge, cure of Izdubar, his lamentation over Heabani.

In this chapter I give under the head of the first tablet an account of my latest conclusions on the subject of the personality of Nimrod, and his identity with the Izdubar of these legends.

TABLET I.

The opening words of the first tablet are preserved, they happen as usual to form the title of the series, but the expressions in the title are obscure, from want of any context to explain them. There are two principal or key words, *naqbi* and *kugar*; the meaning of *kugar* is quite unknown, and *naqbi* is ambiguous, having several meanings, one being "channel" or "water-course," which I have before conceived to be its meaning here; but it has another meaning, which I now think better fits the character of the legends, this meaning is "curse" or "misfortune." Taking this meaning, the opening line will read as the title of the legends, "Of the misfortune seen to happen to Izdubar." This makes the legends the story of a curse or misfortune which befell the great Babylonian king Izdubar; and, now that the fragments are put together and arranged in order, it appears that this is a correct description of the contents of these curious tablets.

After the heading and opening line there is a considerable blank in the story, two columns of writing being entirely lost. It is probable that this part contained the account of the parentage and previous history of Izdubar, forming the introduction to the story. In the subsequent portions of the history there is very little information to supply the loss of this part of the inscription; but it appears that the mother of Izdubar was named Dannat, which is only a title meaning "lady" or "wife of the chief." His father is not named in any of our present fragments, but he is referred to in the third tablet. He is most probably represented to be a god, and the most likely deity is Samas, who is supposed to interfere very much in his behalf. It was a common idea of antiquity, that men who distinguished themselves very much, although born of earthly mothers, had divine fathers. Izdubar, whose parentage, like that of so many heroes of antiquity, is thus doubtful, appears as a mighty leader, a man strong in war and hunting, a giant who gained dominion in Babylonia. The whole of the Euphrates valley was at this time divided into petty kingdoms, and Izdubar by his prowess established a dominion over many of these, making thus the first empire in Asia.

The centre of the empire of Izdubar appears to have laid in the region of Shinar, at Babylon, Akkad, Erech, and Nipur, and agrees with the site of the kingdom of Nimrod, according to Genesis x. 8, 9, 10, where we read: "And Cush begat Nimrod: he began to be a mighty one in the earth. He was a mighty hunter before the Lord: wherefore it is said, even as Nimrod the mighty hunter before the Lord. And the beginning of his kingdom was Babel, and Erech, and Accad, and Calneh, in the land of Shinar." All these cities were ultimately within the dominion of Izdubar, whose character as hunter, leader, and king corresponds with that of Nimrod, and the name of Shamas, or Samas the sun-god, who is most probably represented as his father, may read Kusu, the same name as that of the father of Nimrod.

The next passage in Genesis after the one describing Nimrod's dominion also in my opinion refers to Nimrod, and relates the extension of his kingdom into Assyria. Our version makes Assur the moving party here, but I prefer to read with the margin, "Out of that land he went forth to Assyria," instead of "Out of that land went forth Assur." These verses will then read (Genesis, x. 11, 12): "Out of that land he went forth to Assyria, and builded Nineveh, and Rehobothair, and Calah, and Resen, between Nineveh and Calah: the same is a great city."

As my identification of Izdubar with Nimrod has met with some objection, I think it will be useful to notice the various accounts of this hero, and the different hypotheses propounded with respect to his identification.

The two passages already quoted from Genesis afford the only reliable information with respect to Nimrod outside the cuneiform inscriptions. According to Genesis Nimrod was a "son of Cush," that is a Cushite, or Ethiopian, and he distinguished himself as a mighty hunter, his prowess being so great that his name passed into a proverb. He afterwards became king, commencing his reign in Shinar or Babylonia, and still later extended his empire into Assyria, where he laid the foundations of that state by the foundation of the four leading cities, Nineveh, Calah, Rehobothair, and Resen. The fame of Nimrod is again alluded to in the Bible, where Assyria is called the land of Nimrod.

After the date of the later books of the Old Testament we know nothing of Nimrod for some time; it is probable that he was fully mentioned by Berosus in his history, but his account of the giant hunter has been lost. The reason of this appears to be, that a false idea had grown up among early Christian writers that the Biblical Nimrod was the first king of Babylonia after the Flood, and looking at the list of Berosus they found that after the Flood according to him Evechous first reigned in Babylonia, and they at once assumed that the Evechous of Berosus was the Nimrod of the Bible, and as Evechous has given to him the extravagant reign of four ners or 2,400 years, and his son and successor, Chomasbelus, four ners and five sosses, or 2,700 years, this identification gives little hope of finding an historical Nimrod.

It is most probable that this false identification of Nimrod with Evechous, made by the early chronologists, has caused them to overlook his name and true epoch in the list of Berosus, and has thus lost to us his position in the series of Babylonian sovereigns.

Belonging to the first centuries of the Christian era are the works of various Jewish and Christian writers, who have made us familiar with a number of later traditions of Nimrod. Josephus declares that he was a prime mover in building the Tower of Babel, an enemy of God, and that he reigned at Babylon during the dispersion. Later writers make him contemporary with Abraham, the inventor of idol worship, and a furious worshipper of fire. At the city of Orfa, in Syria, he is said to have cast Abraham into a burning fiery furnace because he would not bow down to his idols. These traditions have been taken up by the Arabs, and although his history has been lost and replaced by absurd and worthless stories Nimrod still remains the most prominent name in the traditions of the country; everything good or evil is attributed to him, and the most important ruins are even now called after his name. From the time of the early Christian writers down to to-day, men have been busy framing systems of general chronology, and as Nimrod was always known as a famous sovereign it was necessary to find a definite place for him in any chronological scheme. Africanus and Eusebius held that he was the Evechous of Berosus, and reigned first after the Flood. Moses of Khorene identified him with Bel, the great god of Babylon; and he is said to have extended his dominions to the foot of the Armenian mountains, falling in battle there when attempting to enforce his authority over Haic, king of Armenia. Some other writers identified Nimrod with Ninus, the mythical founder of the city of Nineveh. These remained the principal identifications before modern research took up the matter; but so wide a door was open to conjecture, that one writer actually identified Nimrod with the Alorus of Berosus, the first king of Babylonia before *the* Flood.

One of the most curious theories about Nimrod, suggested in modern times, was grounded on the "Book of Nabatean Agriculture." This work is a comparatively modern forgery, pretending to be a literary production of the early Chaldean period. What grounds there may be for any of its statements I do not know; but it is possible that some of the book may be compiled from traditions now lost. In this work, Nimrod heads a list of Babylonian kings called Canaanite, and a writer, whose name is unknown to me, argued with considerable. force in favour of these Canaanites being the Arabs of Berosus, who reigned about B.C. 1550 to 1300. Part of Arabia was certainly Cushite, and, as Nimrod is called a Cushite in Genesis, there was a great temptation to identify him with the leader of the Arab dynasty. This idea, however, gained little favour, and has not, I think, been held by any section of inquirers as fixing the position of Nimrod. The discovery of the cuneiform inscriptions threw a new light on the subject of Babylonian history, and soon after the decipherment of the inscriptions attention was directed to the question of the identity and age of Nimrod. Sir Henry Rawlinson, the father of Assyrian discovery, first seriously attempted to fix the name of Nimrod in the cuneiform inscriptions, and he endeavoured to find the name in that of the second god of the great Chaldean triad. (See Rawlinson's "Ancient Monarchies," vol. i. p. 117.) The names of this deity are really Enu, Elu, Kaptu, and Bel, and he was evidently worshipped at the dawn of Babylonian history, in fact he is represented as one of the creators of the world; beside which, time has shown that the cuneiform characters on which the identification was grounded do not bear the phonetic values then supposed.

Sir Henry Rawlinson also suggested ("Ancient Monarchies," p. 136) that the god Nergal was a deification of Nimrod. Sir Henry rightly explains Her-gal as meaning " great man," and his character as a warrior and hunter-god is similar to that of Nimrod, but even if Nimrod was deified under the name of Nergal this does not explain his position or epoch.

Canon Rawlinson, brother of Sir Henry, in the first volume of his "Ancient Monarchies," p. 153, and following, makes some judicious remarks on the chronological position of Nimrod, and suggests that he may have reigned a century or two before B.C. 2286; he also recognizes the historical character of his reign, and supposes him to have founded the Babylonian monarchy, but he does not himself identify him with any king known from the inscriptions. At the time when this was written (1871), the conclusions of Canon Rawlinson were the most satisfactory that had been advanced since the discovery of the cuneiform inscriptions. Since this time, however, some new theories have been started, with the idea of identifying Nimrod; one of these, brought forward by Professor Oppert, makes the word a geographical name, but such an explanation is evidently quite insufficient to account for the traditions attached to the name.

Another theory brought forward by the Rev. A. H. Sayce and Josef Grivel, "Transactions of Society of Biblical Archæology," vol. ii. part 2, p.243, and vol. iii. part 1, p. 136, identifies Nimrod with Merodach, the god of Babylon; but, beside other objections, we have the fact that Merodach was considered by the Babylonians to have been one of the creators of the world, and therefore they could not have supposed him to be a deified king whose reign was after the Flood. I have always felt that Nimrod, whose name figures so prominently in Eastern tradition, and whose reign is clearly stated in Genesis, ought to be found somewhere in the cuneiform text, but I first inclined to the mistaken idea that he might be Hammurabi, the first Arab king of Berosus, as this line of kings appeared to be connected with the Cosseans. This identification failing, I was entirely in the dark until I discovered the Deluge tablet in 1872, I then conjectured that the hero whose name I provisionally called Izdubar was the Nimrod of the Bible, a conjecture which I have strengthened by fresh evidence from time to time.

Considering that Nimrod was the most famous of the Babylonian kings in tradition, it is evident that no history of the country can be complete without some notice of him. His absence from previous histories, and the unsatisfactory theories which have been propounded to account for it, serve to show the difficulties which surround his identification.

The supposition that Nimrod was an ethnic or geographical name, which was slightly favoured by Sir Henry Rawlinson, and has since been urged by Professor Oppert, is quite untenable, for it would be impossible on this theory to account for the traditions which spread abroad with regard to Nimrod.

The idea that Nimrod was Bel, or Elu, the second god in the great Babylonian triad, was equally impossible for the same reason, and because the worship of Bel was, as I have already stated, much more ancient, he being considered one of the creators of the universe and the father of the gods. Bel was the deification of the powers of nature on earth, just as Anu was a deification of the powers of nature in heaven. Similar objections apply to the supposition that Nimrod was Merodach, the god of Babylon, and to his identification with Nergal, who was the man-headed lion. Of course Nimrod was deified like several other celebrated kings, but in no case was a deified king invested as one of the supreme gods and represented as a creator; such a process could only come if a nation entirely forgot its history, and lost its original mythology.

My own opinion that he was the hero I have hitherto called Izdubar was first founded on the discovery that he formed the centre of the national historical poetry, and was the hero of Babylonian cuneiform history, just as Nimrod is stated to have been in the later traditions.

I subsequently found that he agreed exactly in character with Nimrod; he was a giant hunter, according to the cuneiform legends, who contended with and destroyed the lion, tiger, leopard, and wild bull or buffalo, animals the most formidable in the chase in any country. He ruled first in Babylonia over the region which from other sources we know to have been the centre of Nimrod's kingdom. He extended his dominion to the Armenian mountains, the boundary of his late conquests according to tradition, and one principal scene of his exploits and triumphs was the city of Erech, which, according to Genesis, was the second capital of Nimrod.

There remains the fact that the cuneiform name of this hero is undeciphered, the name Izdubar, which I applied to him, being, as I have always stated, a makeshift, only adhered to because some scholars were reluctant to believe he was Nimrod, and I thought it better to continue the use of a name which did not prejudice the question of his identity, and could consequently be used by all irrespective of their opinions. My own conviction is, however, that when the phonetic reading of the characters is found it will turn out to correspond with the name Nimrod. I have already evidence for applying this reading to the characters, but it is impossible to give the proofs in a popular work like the present. I believe that the translations and notes given in this book will lead to the general admission of the identity of the hero I call Izdubar with the traditional Nimrod, and when this result is established I shall myself abandon the provisional name Izdubar, which cannot possibly be correct.

At the time of the opening of this story, the great city of the south of Babylonia, and the capital of this part of the country, was Uruk or Aruk, called, in the Genesis account of Nimrod, Erech. Erech was devoted to the worship of Anu, god of heaven, and his wife, the goddess Anatu, and was ruled at this time by a queen named Istar or Ishtar, who was supposed to be daughter of Anu and Anatu. Istar had been the wife of the chief of Erech, Dumuzi (the Tammuz of the Greeks), who like her was afterwards deified. On the death of Dumuzi, Ishtar had ruled at Erech, and according to the accounts had indulged in a dissolute course of life, which was the scandal of the whole country.

Here I provisionally place the first fragment of the Izdubar legends, K 3200. This fragment consists of part of the third column of a tablet, I believe of the first tablet; and it gives an account of a conquest of Erech by some enemy, which happened during the time of Istar and Izdubar. This fragment reads:—

1. his . . . . . he left
2. his . . . . . went down to the river,
3. in the river his ships were placed.
4. . . . were . . . . and wept bitterly
5. . . . placed, the city of Ganganna was powerless.
6. . . . their . . . . she asses
7. . . . their . . . . great.
8. Like animals the people feared,
9. like doves the slaves mourned.
10. The gods of Erech Suburi
11. turned to flies and fled away in droves.
12. The spirits of Erech Suburi
13. turned to Sikkim and went out in companies.
14. For three years the city of Erech could not resist the enemy,
15. the great gates were thrown down and trampled upon,
16. the goddess Istar before her enemies could not lift her head.
17. Bel his mouth opened and spake,
18. to Ishtar the queen a speech he made:
19. . . . in the midst of Nipur my hands have placed,
20. . . . my country? Babylon the house of my delight,

21. and my people? my hands have given.

22. . . . he looked at the sanctuaries

23. . . . in the day

24. . . . the great gods.

Here we have a graphic account of the condition of Erech, when the enemy overran the country, and the first question which occurs is, who were these conquerors? My original idea was that they were a tribe who held Erech for a short time, and were driven out by Izdubar, whose exploit and subsequent assumption of the crown of Erech were related in the remainder of the first tablet (see "Assyrian Discoveries," p. 169), but this conjecture has not been confirmed by my subsequent investigations; in fact it appears that Izdubar did not assume the crown until long after the events recorded on this tablet. It appears that Izdubar did not become king until after he had slain the tyrant Humbaba, and this leads directly to the conclusion that it was Humbaba, or at least the race to which he belonged, that conquered and tyrannized over Erech and probably over the whole of Babylonia.

The name of Humbaba, or Hubaba, as it is occasionally written, is evidently Elamite and composed of two elements, "Humba," the name of a celebrated Elamite god, and "ba," a verb, usually a contraction for ban, bana, and bani, meaning "to make," the whole name meaning "Humbaba has made [me]." Many other Elamite names compounded with Humba are mentioned in the inscriptions: Humba-sidir, an early chief; Humba-undasa, an Elamite general opposed to Sennacherib; Humba-nigas, an Elamite monarch opposed to Sargon; Tul-humba, an Elamite city, &c.

The notice of foreign dominion, and particularly of Elamite supremacy at this time, may, I think, form a clue from which to ascertain the approximate age of Izdubar; but I would first guard against the impression that the Elamites of this age were the same race as the Elamites known in later times. It is probable that new waves of conquest and colonization passed over all these regions between the time of Izdubar and the Assyrian period, although the same deities continued to be adored in the countries.

Looking at the fragments of Berosus and the notices of Greek and Roman authors, the question now arises, is there any epoch of conquest and foreign dominion which can approximately be fixed upon as the era of Izdubar? I think there is.

The earlier part of the list of Berosus gives the following dynasties or, more properly, periods from the Flood downwards:—

86 Chaldean kings reigned from the Flood down to the Median conquest, 34,080 or 33,091 years.

8 Median kings who conquered and held Babylon, 234, or 224, or 190 years.

11 other kings, race and duration unknown.

49 Chaldean kings, 458 years.

The last of these dynasties, the 49 kings, reigned, as I have already pointed out, from about B.C. 2000 to 1550, and throughout their time the Izdubar legends were known, and allusions to them are found. The time of Izdubar must therefore be before their period, and, as he headed a native rule after a period of conquest, the only possible place for him, according to our present knowledge, is at the head of the 11 kings, and succeeding the Medes of Berosus.

This position for Izdubar or Nimrod, if it should turn out correct, will guide us to several valuable conclusions as to Babylonian history. So far as the dynasty is concerned, which Berosus calls Median, it is most probable that these kings were Elamites; certainly we have no knowledge of the Arian Medes being on the Assyrian frontier until several centuries later, and it is generally conceded that Berosus, in calling them Medes, has only expressed their Eastern origin. Allowing them to be Elamites, or inhabitants of Elam, there remains the question, to what race did they belong?

The later Elamites are believed to have been either Turanians or Arians; but we are by no means certain that no new race had come into the country since the time of Izdubar. There was a constant stream of immigration from the east and north, which gradually but surely altered the character of several of the races of Western Asia.

In Babylonia itself it is believed that a change of this sort took place in early times, the original Turanian population having been conquered and enslaved by Semitic tribes, and there has always been a difficulty as to where the Semitic peoples originated.

The Semitic race was already dominant in Babylonia two thousand years before the Christian era, and before this time there is only one conquest recorded—that of Babylonia by the Medes or Elamites, and I think it is most likely that from Elam the Semites first came. The usual theory is that the Semitic race came from Arabia; but this is quite unlikely, as there is no known conquest of Babylonia from this direction previous to the sixteenth century before the Christian era.

In the Book of Genesis Elam is counted as the first son of Shem or Semitic nation, and I think this may indicate a knowledge, at the time that book was written, that the Semitic race came from this direction; they were probably driven westward by the advance of the Arians, and these latter in their progress may have obliterated nearly all the traces of the Semites whom they dispossessed.

The next question which strikes an observer is as to the date of these events. Some years back I published a curious inscription, of which I gave the texts and translations in my "History of Assurbanipal," pp. 234 to 251, referring to the goddess Nana, the Ishtar of Erech, also called Uzur-amat-sa. In these inscriptions a period of 1635 is mentioned as ending at the capture of Shushan, the capital of Elam, by the Assyrians, about B.C. 645, thus making the initial date B.C. 2280. At that time an image of Nana was carried into captivity from Erech by the Elamite king, Kudur-nanhundi, who, according to these inscriptions, appears to have then ruled over and oppressed the land of Babylonia. It is possible that the ravaging of the city of Erech, mentioned in the fragment of the first tablet of the Izdubar legends, recounts the very event alluded to by Assurbanipal. This date and the circumstances of the Elamite conquest form, I think, a clue to the age of Izdubar. Kudur-nanhundi, who plundered Erech, was probably one of the later kings of this dynasty, and Humba-ba was the last. A fragment which refers to this period in " Cuneiform Inscriptions," vol. iii. p. 38, relates the destruction wrought in the country by the Elamites, and gives Kudur-nanhundi as following one of the other monarchs of this line, and as exceeding his predecessors in the injury he did to the country.

Putting together the detached notices of this period, I conjecture the following to be somewhere about the chronology, the dates being understood as round numbers.

B.C. 2450, Elamites overrun Babylonia.

B.C. 2280, Kudur-nanhundi, king of Elam, ravages Erech.

B.C. 2250, Izdubar or Nimrod slays Humba-ba, and restores the Chaldean power.

There is one serious objection to this idea. Although the date B.C. 2280 appears to be given in the inscription of Assurbanipal for the ravages of Kudur-nanhundi, yet the other mutilated notices of this Elamite monarch are combined with names of Babylonian monarchs who do not appear to be anything like so ancient. One of these, said in the inscription, "Cuneiform Inscriptions," vol. iii. p. 38, No. 2, to be contemporary with Kudur-nanhundi, is Bel-zakir-uzur. No name compounded in this form has yet been found earlier than B.C. 1500.

Although the dates transmitted through ancient authors are as a rule vague and doubtful, there are many independent notices which seem to point to somewhere about the twenty-third century before the Christian era for the foundation of the Babylonian and Assyrian power. Several of these dates are connected either directly or by implication with Nimrod, who first formed a united empire over these regions.

The following are some of these notices:—

Simplicius relates that Callisthenis, the friend of Alexander, sent to Aristotle from Babylon a series of stellar observations reaching back 1,903 years before the taking of Babylon by Alexander. This would make 1903 + 331 = B.C. 2234.

Philo-biblius, according to Stephen, made the foundation of Babylon 1,002 years before Semiramis and the Trojan war, as these later were supposed to have been in the thirteenth century B.C. This comes to about the same date.

Berosus and Critodemus are said by Pliny to have made the inscribed stellar observations reach to 480 years before the era of Phoroneus; the latter date was supposed to be about the middle of the eighteenth century B.C., 480 years before it, comes also to about the same date.

These three instances are given in Rawlinson's "Ancient Monarchies," p. 149.

Diodorus makes the Assyrian empire commence a thousand years or more before the Trojan war.

Ctesius and Cephalion make its foundation early in the twenty-second century B.C.

Auctor Barbarus makes it in the twenty-third century B.C.

These and other notices probably point to about the same period, the time when Nimrod united Babylonia into one monarchy, and founded Nineveh in Assyria.

Before parting with the consideration of the first tablet, I will give a small fragment, which I provisionally insert here for want of a better place.

1. . . . to thee . . . . .
2. Bel thy father sent me . . . .
3. thus . . . . heard . . . .
4. When in the midst of those forests . . . .
5. he rejoiced at its fragrance and . . . .

6. at first . . . . .

p. 192

7. Go and thou shalt take . . . .

8. Mayest thou rejoice . . . .

Of the latter part of the first tablet we have as yet no knowledge.

CHAPTER XII: MEETING OF HEABANI AND IZDUBAR.

Dream of Izdubar.—Heabani.—His wisdom.—His solitary life.— Izdubar's petition.—Zaidu.—Harimtu and Samhat.—Tempt Heabani.—Might and fame of Izdubar.—Speech of Heabani.—His journey to Erech.—The midannu or tiger.—Festival at Erech.— Dream of Izdubar.—Friendship with Heabani.

IN this chapter I have included the fragments of what appear to be the second and third tablets. In this section of the story Izdubar comes prominently forward, and meets with Heabani. I have already noticed the supposed parentage of Izdubar; the notice of his mother Dannat appears in one of the tablets given in this chapter.

Izdubar, in the Babylonian and Assyrian sculptures, is always represented with a marked physiognomy. He is indicated as a man with masses of curls over his head and a large curly beard. So marked is this, and different in cast to the usual Babylonian type, that I cannot help the impression of its being a representation of a distinct and probably Ethiopian type.

The deity of Izdubar was Sarturda, from which I suppose he was a native of the district of Amarda or Marad, where that god was worshipped. This district was probably the Amordacia or Mardocæa of Ptolemy, but I do not know where it was situated.

The fragments of the second and third tablets assume by their notices that Izdubar was already known as a mighty hunter, and it appeared a little later that he claimed descent from the old Babylonian kings, calling Hasisadra his "father."

TABLET II.

I have recovered a single fragment, which I believe to belong to this tablet; it is K 3389, and it contains part of the third and fourth columns of writing. It appears from this that Izdubar was then at Erech, and he had a curious dream. He thought he saw the stars of heaven fall to the ground, and in their descent they struck upon his back. He then saw standing over him a terrible being, the aspect of his face was fierce, and he was armed with claws, like the claws of lions. The greater part of the description of the dream is lost; it probably occupied columns I. and II. of the second tablet. Thinking that the dream portended some fate to himself, Izdubar calls on all the wise men to explain it, and offers a reward to any one who can interpret the dream. Here the fragment Ii 3389 comes in:

COLUMN III.

1. . . . . ru kili I . . . .
2. . . . . he and the princes may he . . .
3. . . . . in the vicinity send him,
4. . . . . may they ennoble his family,
5. . . . . at the head of his feast may he set thee
6. . . . . may he array thee in jewels and gold
7. . . . . may he enclose thee
8. . . . . in his . . . . seat thee
9. into the houses of the gods may he cause thee to enter
10. . . . . seven wives
11. . . . . cause illness in his stomach
12. . . . . went up alone
13. . . . . his heaviness to his friend
14. . . . . a dream I dreamed in my sleep
15. . . . . the stars of heaven fell to the earth
16. . . . . I stood still
17. . . . . his face
18. . . . . his face was terrible
19. . . . . like the claws of a lion, were his claws
20. . . . . the strength in me
21. . . . . he slew
22. . . . . me
23. . . . . over me
24. . . . . corpse . . . .

The first part of this fragment appears to contain the honours offered by Izdubar to any one who should interpret the dream. These included the ennobling of his family, his recognition in assemblies, his being invested with jewels of honour, and his wives being increased. A description of the dream of the hero, much mutilated, follows. The conduct of Nebuchadnezzar in the Book of Daniel, with reference to his dreams, bears some resemblance to that of Izdubar.

After this fragment we have again a blank in the story, and it would appear that in this interval application was made to a hermit named

Heabani that he would go to the city of Erech and interpret the dream of Izdubar.

Heabani appears, from the representations on seals and other objects on which he is figured, to have been a satyr or faun. He is always drawn with the feet and tail of an ox, and with horns on his head. He is said to have lived in a cave among the wild animals of the forest, and was supposed to possess wonderful knowledge both of nature and human affairs. Heabani was angry at the request that he should abandon his solitary life for the friendship of Izdubar, and where our narrative reopens the god Samas is persuading him to accept the offer.

COLUMN IV.

1. . . . . me
2. . . . . on my back

---

3. And Shamas opened his mouth
4. and spake and from heaven said to him:
5. . . . . and the female Samhat (delightful) thou shalt choose
6. they shall array thee in trappings of divinity
7. they shall give thee the insignia of royalty
8. they shall make thee become great
9. and Izdubar thou shalt call and incline him towards thee
10. and Izdubar shall make friendship unto thee
11. he shall cause thee to recline on a grand couch
12. on a beautiful couch he shall seat thee
13. he will cause thee to sit on a comfortable seat a seat on the left
14. the kings of the earth shall kiss thy feet
15. he shall enrich thee and the men of Erech he shall make silent before thee
16. and he after thee shall take all . . . .
17. he shall clothe thy body in raiment and . . . .

---

18. Heabani heard the words of Shamas the warrior
19. and the anger of his heart was appeased
20. . . . . was appeased

Here we are still dealing with the honours which Izdubar promises to the interpreter of his dream, and these seem to show that Izdubar had some power at Erech at this time; he does not, however, appear to have been an independent king, and it is probable that the next two columns of this tablet, now lost, contain negotiations for bringing Heabani to Erech, the subject being continued on the third tablet.

TABLET III.

This tablet is far better preserved than the two previous ones; it gives the account of the successful mission to bring Heabani to Ur, opening with a broken account of the wisdom of Heabani.

COLUMN I.

1. . . . . knows all things
2. . . . . and difficult
3. . . . . wisdom of all things
4. . . . . the knowledge that is seen and that which is hidden
5. . . . . bring word of peace to . . .
6. from a far off road he will come and I rest and. . . .
7. . . . . on tablets and all that rests . . .
8. . . . . and tower of Erech Suburi
9. . . . . beautiful
10. . . . . which like . . . .
11. . . . . I strove with him not to leave . . . .
12. . . . . god? who from . . . .
13. . . . . carry . . . .
14. . . . . leave . . . .

(Many lines lost.)

COLUMN II.

1. Izdubar did not leave . . . .
2. Daughter of a warrior . . . .
3. their might . . . .
4. the gods of heaven, lord . . . .
5. thou makest to be sons and family? . . . .
6. there is not any other like thee . . . .
7. in the depth made . . . .
8. Izdubar did not leave, the son to his father day and night . . . .
9. he the ruler also of Erech . . . .
10. he their ruler and . . . .
11. made firm? and wise . . . .
12. Izdubar did not leave Dannat, the son to his mother . . . .
13. Daughter of a warrior, wife of . . . .
14. their might the god . . . . heard and . . . .
15. Aruru strong and great, thou Aruru hast made . . . .

16. again making his strength, one day his heart . . . . . .

17. he changed and the city of Erech . . . . . .

18. Aruru on hearing this, the strength of Anu made in the midst . . . . . .

19. Aruru put in her hands, she bowed her breast and lay on the ground

20. . . . Heabani she made a warrior, begotten of the seed of the soldier Ninip

21. . . . . . covered his body, retiring in companionship like a woman,

22. the features of his aspect were concealed like the corn god

23. possessing knowledge of men and countries, in clothing clothed like the god Ner

24. with the gazelles he eat food in the night

25. with the beasts of the field he consorted in the day

26. with the creeping things of the waters his heart delighted

27. Zaidu catcher of men

28. in front of that field confronted him

29. the first day the second day and the third in the front of that field the same

30. the courage of Zaidu dried up before him

31. and he and his beast entered into his house and

32. . . . . fear dried up and overcome

33. . . . . his courage grew before him

34. . . . . his face was terrible

COLUMN III.

1. Zaidu opened his mouth and spake and said to . . . . .

2. My father the first leader who shall go . . . . .

3. in the land of . . . . .

4. like the soldier of Anu . . . . .

5. shall march over the country . . . . .

6. and firmly with the beast . . . . .

7. and firmly his feet in the front of the field . . .

8. I feared and I did not approach it

9. he filled the cave which he had dug

10. . . . . . .

11. I ascended on my hands to the . . . .

12. I did not reach to the . . . . .

---

13. . . . . and said to Zaidu

14. . . . . Erech, Izdubar
15. . . . . ascend his field
16. . . . . his might
17. . . . . thy face
18. . . . . the might of a man
19. . . . .
20. . . . . like a chief
21. . . . . field
22 to 24 three lines of directions
25. According to the advice of his father . . . .
26. Zaidu went . . . .
27. he took the road and in the midst of Erech he halted
28. . . . . Izdubar . . . .
29. the first leader who shall go . . . .
30. in the land of . . . .
31. like the soldier of Anu . . . .
32. shall march over the country . . . .
33. and firmly with the beast . . . .
34. and firmly his feet . . . .
35. I feared and I did not approach it
36. he filled the cave which he had dug
37. . . . . . .
38. I ascended on my hands . . . . .
39. I was not able to reach to the covert.
40. Izdubar to him also said to Zaidu:
41. go Zaidu and with thee the female Harimtu, and Samhat take,
42. and when the beast . . . in front of the field

---

43 to 45. directions to the female how to entice Heabani.
46. Zaidu went and with him Harimtu, and Samhat he took, and
47. they took the road, and went along the path.
48. On the third day they reached the land where the flood happened.
49. Zaidu and Harimtu in their places sat,
50. the first day and the second day in front of the field they sat,
51. the land where the beast drank of drink,
COLUMN IV.
1. the land where the creeping things of the water rejoiced his heart.
2. And he Heabani had made for himself a mountain

3. with the gazelles he eat food,

4. with the beasts he drank of drink,

5. with the creeping things of the waters his heart rejoiced.

6. Samhat the enticer of men saw him

7 to 26. details of the actions of the female Sam-hat and Heabani.

27. And Heabani approached Harimtu then, who before had not enticed him.

28. And he listened . . . . and was attentive,

29. and he turned and sat at the feet of Harimtu.

30. Harimtu bent down her face,

31. and Harimtu spake; and his ears heard

32. and to him also she said to Heabani:

33. Famous Heabani like a god art thou,

34. Why dost thou associate with the creeping things in the desert?

35. I desire thy company to the midst of Erech Suburi,

36. to the temple of Elli-tardusi the seat of Anu and Ishtar,

37. the dwelling of Izdubar the mighty giant,

38. who also like a bull towers over the chiefs.

39. She spake to hint and before her speech,

40. the wisdom of his heart flew away and disappeared.

41. Heabani to her also said to Harimtu:

42. I join to Samhat my companionship,

43. to the temple of Elli-tardusi the seat of Anu and Ishtar,

44. the dwelling of Izdubar the mighty giant,

45. who also like a bull towers over the chiefs.

46. I will meet him and see his power,

COLUMN V.

1. I will bring to the midst of Erech a tiger,

2. and if he is able he will destroy it.

3. In the desert it is begotten, it has great strength,

4. . . . . before thee

5. . . . . everything there is I know

6. Heabani went to the midst of Erech Suburi

7. . . . . . the chiefs . . . made submission

8. in that day they made a festival

9. . . . . . city

10. . . . . . daughter

11. . . . . . made rejoicing

12. . . . . becoming great
13. . . . . mingled and
14. . . . . Izdubar rejoicing the people
15. went before him
16. A prince thou becomest glory thou hast
17. . . . . fills his body
18. . . . . who day and night
19. . . . . destroy thy terror
20. . . . . the god Samas loves him and
21. . . . . and Hea have given intelligence to his ears
22. he has come from the mountain
23. to the midst of Erech he will ponder thy dream
24. Izdubar his dream revealed and said to his mother
25. A dream I dreamed in my sleep
26. . . . . the stars of heaven
97. . . . . struck upon my back
28. . . . . of heaven over me
29. . . . . did not rise over it
p. 205
30. . . . . stood over . . . . .
31. . . . . him and
32. . . . . over him
33. . . . . his . . . .
34. . . . . . . .princess
35. . . . . me
36. . . . . I know
37. . . . . to Izdubar
38. . . . . of heaven
39. . . . . over thy back
40. . . . . over thee
41. . . . . did not rise over it
42. . . . . my . . . . .
43. . . . . thee

There is one other mutilated fragment of this and the next column with part of a relation respecting beasts and a fragment of a conversation between Izdubar and his mother.

The whole of this tablet is curious, and it certainly gives the successful issue of the attempt to bring Heabani to Erech, and in very fragmentary condition the dream of the monarch.

I have omitted some of the details in columns III. and IV. because they were on the one side obscure, and on the other hand appeared hardly adapted for general reading.

It appears that the females Samhat and Harimtu prevailed upon Heabani to come to Erech and see the exploits of the giant Izdubar, and he declared that he would bring a *Midannu*, most probably a tiger, to Erech, in order to make trial of the strength of Izdubar, and to see if he could destroy it.

The Midannu is mentioned in the Assyrian texts as a fierce carnivorous animal allied to the lion and leopard; it is called *Midannu*, Mindinu, and Mandinu.

In the fifth column, after the description of the festivities which followed the arrival of Heabani, there appears a break between lines 15 and 16, some part of the original story being probably omitted here. I believe that the Assyrian copy is here defective, at least one line being lost. The portion here omitted probably stated that the following speech was made by the mother of Izdubar, who figures prominently in the earlier part of these legends.

CHAPTER XIII: DESTRUCTION OF THE TYRANT HUMBABA.

**Elamite dominion.—Forest region.—Humbaba.—Conversation.—
Petition to Shamas.—Journey to forest.—Dwelling of Humbaba.—
Entrance to forest.—Meeting with Humbaba.—Death of Humbaba.—
Izdubar king.**

I HAVE had considerable difficulty in writing this chapter; in fact I have arranged the matter now three times, and such is the wretched broken condition of the fragments that I am even now quite uncertain if I have the correct order. The various detached fragments belong to the fourth and fifth tablets in the series, and relate the contest between Izdubar and Humbaba.

I have already stated my opinion that Humbaba was an Elamite, and that he was the last of the dynasty which, according to Berosus, conquered and held Babylonia for about two centuries, between B.C. 2450 and 2250. Humbaba held his court in the midst of a region of *erini* trees, where there were also trees of the specie called *Survan*; these two words are very vaguely used in the inscriptions, and appear to refer rather to the quality and appearance of the trees than to the exact species. *Erini* is used for a tall fine tree: it is used for the pine, cedar, and ash. I have here translated the word "pine," and *survan* I have translated "cedar." In one inscription Lebanon is said to be the country of *survan*, in allusion to its cedar trees.

This section of the Izdubar legends was undoubtedly of great importance, for, although it was disfigured by the poetical adornments deemed necessary to give interest to the narrative, yet of itself, as it described the overthrow of a dynasty and the accession of Izdubar to the throne, it has interest for us in spite of its mutilated condition. When I published my "Assyrian Discoveries" none of these fragments were in condition for publication, but I have since joined and restored some of them, and the new fragments have given sufficient aid to enable me now to present them in some sort, but it is quite possible that any further accession of new fragments would alter the arrangement I have here given.

I at first placed in this division a fragment of the story made up from three parts of a tablet, and containing a discourse of Heabani to some trees, but subsequent investigation has caused me to withdraw this fragment and place it in the space of the eighth tablet.

In the case of the fourth tablet I think I have fragments of all six columns, but some of these fragments are useless until we have further fragments to complete them.

TABLET IV.

COLUMN I.

1. . . . . . mu . . . .
2. . . . . . thy. . . .
3. . . . . . me, return
4. . . . . . the birds shall rend him
5. . . . . . in thy presence
6. . . . . . of the forest of pine trees
7. . . . . . all the battle
8. . . . . . may the birds of prey surround him
9. . . . . . that, his carcass may they destroy
10. . . . . . to me and we will appoint thee king,
11. . . . . . thou shalt direct after the manner of a king

---

12. [Izdubar] opened his mouth and spake,
13. and said to Heabani:
14. . . . he goes to the great palace
15. . . . . . the breast of the great queen
16. . . . . . . knowledge, everything he knows
17. . . . . establish to our feet
18. . . . . his hand
19. . . . . I to the great palace
20. . . . . .the great queen
(Probably over twenty lines lost here.)

It was this fragment, which gives part of the conversation between Heabani and Izdubar previous to the attack on Humbaba, which led me to the opinion that Izdubar was not yet king of Babylonia, for Heabani promises (lines 10 and 11) that they will make Izdubar king when they have slain Humbaba and given his corpse to the vultures (lines 4, 8, and 9).

COLUMN II.

1. . . . . . enter
2. . . . . . he raised
3. . . . . . the ornaments of her . . . .

4. . . . . the ornaments of her breast

5. . . . . and her crown I divided

6. . . . . of the earth he opened

7. he . . . he ascended to the city

8. he went up to the presence of Shamas he made a sacrifice?

9. he built an altar. In the presence of Shamas he lifted his hands:

10. Why hast thou established Izdubar, in thy heart thou hast given him protection,

11. when the son . . . . and he goes

12. on the remote path to Humbaba,

13. A battle he knows not he will confront,

14. an expedition he knows not he will ride to,

15. for long he will go and will return,

16. to take the course to the forest of pine trees,

17. to Humbaba of [whom his city may] he destroy,

18. and every one who is evil whom thou hatest . . .

19. In the day of the year he will . . . .

20. May she not return at all, may she not . . .

21. him to fix . . . .

(About ten lines lost here.)

Here we see that Izdubar, impressed with the magnitude of the task he had undertaken, makes a prayer and sacrifice to Shamas to aid him in his task. The next fragment appears also to belong to this column, and may refer to preliminaries for sacrificing to Ishtar, with a view also to gain her aid in the enterprise.

This fragment of Column II. reads

1. . . . . neighbourhood of Erech . . . .

2. . . . . strong and . . .

3. he burst open the road . . . .

4. and that city . . . .

5. and the collection . . . .

6. placed the people together . . . .

7. the people were ended . . . .

8. like of a king . . . .

9. which for a long time had been made . . . .

10. to the goddess Ishtar the bed . . . .

11. to Izdubar like the god Sakim . . . .

12. Heabani opened the great gate of the house of assembly . . . .

13. for Izdubar to enter . . . .

14. . . . . in the gate of the house . . . .

COLUMN III.

1. the corpse of . . . .

2. to . . . .

3. to the rising of . . .

4. the angels . . . .

5. may she not return . . . .

6. him to fix . . . .

7. the expedition which he knows not . . .

8. may he destroy also . . . .

9. of which he knows . . . .

10. the road . . . . .

Five more mutilated lines, the rest of the column being lost.

This fragment shows Izdubar still invoking the gods for his coming expedition. Under the next column I have placed a fragment, the position and meaning of which are quite unknown.

COLUMN IV.—UNCERTAIN FRAGMENT.

1. he was heavy . . .

2. Heabani was . . . .

3. Heabani strong not rising . . . .

4. When . . . .

5. with thy song? . . . .

6. the sister of the gods faithful . . . .

7. wandering he fixed to . . . .

8. the sister of the gods lifted . . . .

9. and the daughters of the gods grew . . . .

10. I Heabani . . . . he lifted to . . . .

Somewhere here should be the story, now lost, of the starting of Izdubar on his expedition accompanied by his friend Heabani. The sequel shows they arrive at the palace or residence of Heabani, which is surrounded by a forest of pine and cedar, the whole being enclosed by some barrier or wall, with a gate for entrance. Heabani and Izdubar open this gate where the story reopens on the fifth column.

COLUMN V.

1. the sharp weapon

2. to make men fear him . . . .

3. Humbaba poured a tempest out of his mouth . . . .

4. he heard the gate of the forest [open]

5. the sharp weapon to make men fear him [he took]

6. and in the path of his forest he stood and [waited]

---

7. Izdubar to him also [said to Heabani]

Here we see Humbaba waiting for the intruders, but the rest of the column is lost; it appears to have principally consisted of speeches by Izdubar and Heabani on the magnificent trees they saw, and the work before them. A single fragment of Column VI., containing fragments of six lines, shows them still at the gate, and when the next tablet, No. V., opens, they had not yet entered.

TABLET V.

The fifth tablet is more certain than the last; it appears to refer to the conquest of Humbaba or Hubaba. I have only discovered fragments of this tablet, which opens with a description of the retreat of Humbaba.

COLUMN I.

1. He stood and surveyed the forest

2. of pine trees, he perceived its height,

3. of the forest he perceived its approach,

4. in the place where Humbaba went his step was placed,

5. on a straight road and a good path.

6. He saw the land of the pine trees, the seat of the gods, the sanctuary of the angels,

7. in front? of the seed the pine tree carried its fruit,

8. good was its shadow, full of pleasure,

9. an excellent tree, the choice of the forest,

10. . . . . . the pine heaped . . . .

11. . . . . . for one kaspu (7 miles) . .

12. . . . . . cedar two-thirds of it . . .

13. . . . . . grown . .

14. . . . . . like it . . .

. . . .

(About 10 lines lost here.)

25. . . . . . he looked . . . .

26. . . . . . he made and he . . . .

27. . . . . drove to . . . .

28. . . . . he opened and . . . .

---

29. Izdubar opened his mouth and spake, and said to [Heabani]:

30. My friend . . . .

31. . . . . with their slaughter . . . .

32. . . . . he did not speak before her, he made with him . . . .

33. . . . . knowledge of war who made fighting,

34. in entering to the house thou shalt not fear, ...

35. . . . . and like I take her also they . . . .

36. to an end may they seat . . . .

37. . . . . thy hand . . . .

38. . . . . took my friend first . . . .

39. . . . . his heart prepared for war, that year and day also

40. . . . . on his falling appoint the people

41. . . . . slay him, his corpse may the birds of prey surround

42. . . . . of them he shall make

43. . . . . going he took the weight

44. they performed it, their will they established

---

45. . . . . they entered into the forest

COLUMN II.

(Five lines mutilated.)

6. they passed through the forest . . . .

---

7. Humbaba . . . .

8. he did not come . . . .

9. he did not . . . .

(Seven lines lost.)

17. heavy . . . .

18. Heabani opened his mouth . . . .

19. . . . . Humbaba in . . . .

20. . . . one by one and . . . .

(Many other broken lines.)

There are a few fragments of Columns III., IV., and V. and a small portion of Column VI. which reads:

1. . . . . . cedar to . . . .

2. . . . . he placed and . . . .

3. . . . . . 120 . . . . Heabani . . . .

4. . . . . . the head of Humbaba . . . .

---

5. . . . . his weapon he sharpened . . . .

6. . . . . tablet of the story of fate of . . . .

It appears from the various mutilated fragments of this tablet that Izdubar and Heabani conquer and slay Humbaba and take his goods, but much is wanted to connect the fragments.

The conclusion of this stage of the story and triumph of Izdubar are given at the commencement of the sixth tablet. It appears, when the matter is stripped of the marvellous incidents with which the poets have surrounded it, that Izdubar and his friend went privately to the palace of Humbaba, killed the monarch and carried off his regalia, the death of the oppressor being the signal for the proclamation of Babylonian freedom and the reign of Izdubar.

CHAPTER XIV: THE ADVENTURES OF ISHTAR.

Triumph of Izdubar.—Ishtar's love.—Her offer of marriage.—Her promises.—Izdubar's answer.—Tammuz.—Amours of Ishtar.—His refusal.—Ishtar's anger.—Ascends to Heaven.—The bull.—Slain by Izdubar.—Ishtar's curse.—Izdubar's triumph.—The feast.—Ishtar's despair.—Her descent to Hades.—Description.—The seven gates.—The curses.—Uddusunamir.—Sphinx.—Release of Ishtar.—Lament for Tammuz.

IN this section I have included the sixth and seventh tablets, which both primarily refer to the doings of Ishtar.

TABLET VI.

The sixth tablet is in better condition than any of the former ones, and allows of something like a connected translation.

COLUMN I.

1. . . . . his weapon, he sharpened his weapon,
2. Like a bull his country he ascended after him.
3. He destroyed him and his memorial was hidden.
4. The country he wasted, the fastening of the crown he took.
5. Izdubar his crown put on (the fastening of the crown he took).
6. For the favour of Izdubar the princess Ishtar lifted her eyes:
7. I will take thee Izdubar as husband,
8. thy oath to me shall be thy bond,
9. thou shalt be husband and I will be thy wife.
10. Thou shalt drive in a chariot of ukni stone and gold,
11. of which the body is gold and splendid its pole.
12. Thou shalt acquire days of great conquests,
13. to Bitani in the country where the pine trees grow.
14. May Bitani at thy entrance
15. to the river Euphrates kiss thy feet,
16. There shall be under thee kings, lords, and princes.
17. The tribute of the mountains and plains they shall bring to thee, taxes
18. they shall give thee, may thy herds and flocks bring forth twins,
19. . . . . mules be swift
20. . . . . in the chariot strong not weak

21. . . . . in the yoke. A rival may there not be.
22. Izdubar opened his mouth and spake, and
23. said to the princess Ishtar:
24. . . . . to thee thy possession
25. . . . . body and rottenness
26. . . . . baldness and famine
27. . . . . instruments of divinity
28. . . . . instruments of royalty
29. . . . . storm
30. . . . . he poured
31. . . . . was destroyed
32. . . . . thy possession
33. . . . . sent in
34. . . . after . . . . ended wind and showers
35. palace . . . . courage
36. beauty . . . . cover her
37. he said . . . . carry her
38. body glorious . . . . carry her
39. grand . . . . tower of stone
40. let not be placed . . . . land of the enemy
41. body . . . . her lord
42. let them not marry thee . . . . for ever
43. let not praise thee . . . . he ascended
44. I take also the torch? destroy thee
COLUMN II.
1. Which alone . . . . her side
2. to Dumuzi the husband . . . . of thee,
3. country after country mourn his love.
4. The wild eagle also thou didst love and
5. thou didst strike him, and his wings thou didst break;
6. he stood in the forest and begged for his wings.
7. Thou didst love also a lion complete in might,
8. thou didst draw out by sevens his claws.
9. Thou didst love also a horse glorious in war,
10. he poured out to the end and extent his love,
11. After seven kaspu (fourteen hours) his love was not sweet,
12. shaking and tumultuous was his love.
13. To his mother Silele he was weeping for love.

14. Thou didst love also a ruler of the country,

15. and continually thou didst break his weapons.

16. Every day he propitiated thee with offerings,

17. Thou didst strike him and to a leopard thou didst change him,

18. his own city drove him away, and

19. his dogs tore his wounds.

20. Thou didst love also Isullanu the husbandman of thy father,

21. who continually was subject to thy order,

22. and every clay delighted in thy portion.

23. In thy taking him also thou didst turn cruel,

24. Isullanu thy cruelty resisted,

25. and thy hand was brought out and thou didst strike? . . . .

26. Isullanu said to thee:

27. To me why dost thou come

28. mother thou wilt not be and I do not eat,

29. of eaten food for beauty? and charms?

30. trembling and faintness overcome me

31. Thou hearest this . . . .

32. thou didst strike him, and to a pillar? thou didst change him,

33. thou didst place him in the midst of the ground. . . .

34. he riseth not up, he goeth not . . . .

35. And me thou dost love, and like to them thou [wilt serve me].

---

36. Ishtar on her hearing this,

37. Ishtar was angry and to heaven she ascended,

38. and Ishtar went to the presence of Anu her father,

39. to the presence of Anatu her mother she went and said:

40. Father, Izdubar hates me, and

COLUMN III.

1. Izdubar despises my beauty,

2. my beauty and my charms.

---

3. Anu opened his mouth and spake, and

4. said to the princess Ishtar:

5. My daughter thou shalt remove . . . . .

6. and Izdubar will count thy beauty,

7. thy beauty and thy charms.

---

8. Ishtar opened her mouth and spake, and
9. said to Anu her father:
10. My father, create a divine bull and
11. Izdubar . . . .
12. when he is filled . . . .
13. I will strike . . . .
14. I will join . . . .
15. . . . . u. . . . .
16. over . . .

---

17. Anu opened his mouth and spake, and
18. said to the princess Ishtar:
19. . . . . thou shalt join . . . .
20. . . . . of noble names
21. . . . . *mashi* . . . .
22. . . . . which is magnified . . . .

---

23. Ishtar opened her mouth and spake, and
24. said to Anu her father:
25. . . . . I will strike
26. . . . . I will break
27. . . . . . of noble names
28. . . . . reducer
29. . . . . of foods
30. . . . . of him
(Some lines lost here.)
COLUMN IV.
(Some lines lost.)
1. . . . . warriors
2. . . . . to the midst
3. . . . . three hundred warriors
4. . . . . to the midst
5. . . . . slay Heabani
6. in two divisions he parted in the midst of it
7. two hundred warriors . . . . made, the divine bull. . .
8. in the third division . . . . his horns
9. Heabani struck? his might
10. and Heabani pierced . . . . joy . . . .

11. the divine bull by his head he took hold of . . . .

12. the length of his tail . . . .

---

13. Heabani opened his mouth and spake, and

14. said to Izdubar:

15. Friend we will stretch out . . . .

16. then we will overthrow . . . .

17. and the might . . . .

18. may it . . . .

(Three lines lost.)

22. . . . . hands . . . . to Vul and Nebo

23. . . . . *tarka* . . . . *um* . . . .

24. . . . . Heabani took hold . . . . the divine bull

25. . . . . he . . . . also . . . . by his tail

26. . . . . Heabani

COLUMN V.

1. And Izdubar like a . . . .

2. . . . . might and . . . .

3. in the vicinity of the middle of his horns and. . . .

4. from the city he destroyed, the heart . . . .

5. to the presence of Shamas . . . .

6. he had extended to the presence of Shamas. . . . .

7. he placed at the side the bulk . . . .

---

8. And Ishtar ascended unto the wall of Erech Suburi,

9. destroyed the covering and uttered a curse:

10. I curse Izdubar who dwells here, and the winged bull has slain.

11. Heabani heard the speech of Ishtar,

12. and he cut off the member of the divine bull and before her threw it;

13. I answer it, I will take thee and as in this

14. I have heard thee,

15. the curse I will turn against thy side.

16. Ishtar gathered her maidens

17. Samhati and Harimati,

18. and over the member of the divine bull a. mourning she made.

19. Izdubar called on the people . . . .

20. all of them,

21. and the weight of his horns the young men took,

22. 30 manas of zamat stone within them,
23. the sharpness of the points was destroyed,
24. 6 gurs its mass together.
25. To the ark of his god Sarturda he dedicated it;
26. he took it in and worshipped at his fire;
27. in the river Euphrates they washed their hands,
28. and they took and went
29. round the city of Erech riding,
30. and the assembly of' the chiefs of' Erech marked it.
31. Izdubar to the inhabitants of Erech
32. . . . . . a proclamation made.
COLUMN VI.
1. "Any one of ability among the chiefs,
2. Any one noble among men,
3. Izdubar is able among the chiefs,

---

4. Izdubar is noble among men,
5. . . . . . placed hearing
6. . . . . . vicinity, not of the inhabitants
7. . . . . . him."
8. Izdubar in his palace made a rejoicing,
9. the chiefs reclining on couches at night,
10. Heabani lay down, slept, and a dream he dreamed.
11. Heabani spake and the dream he explained,
12. and said to Izdubar.
TABLET VII.
The seventh tablet opens with the words, "Friend why do the gods take council." I am uncertain if I have found any other portion of this tablet, but I have provisionally placed here part of a remarkable fragment, with a continuation of the story of Ishtar. It appears that this goddess, failing in her attempt in heaven to avenge herself on Izdubar for his slight, resolved to descend to hell, to search out, if possible, new modes of attacking him.

Columns I. and II. are lost, the fragments recommencing on column III.
COLUMN III.
1. . . . . . people? to destroy his hand approached
2. . . . . . raise in thy presence
3. . . . . . like before
4. . . . . . Zaidu shall accomplish the wish of his heart

5. with the female Samhat . . . . he takes

6. . . . . thee, the female Samhat will expel thee

7. . . . . ends and . . . . good

8. . . . . kept by the great jailor

9. . . . . like going down they were angry? let them weep for thee

10. . . . goods of the house of thy fullness

11. . . . like death . . . . of thy depression

12. . . . . for the females

13. . . . . let them bow

14. . . . . sink down

15. . . . . those who are collected

16. . . . . she

17. . . . . placed in thy house

18. . . . . occupy thy seat

19. . . . . thy resting place

20. . . . . thy feet

21. . . . . may they destroy

22. . . . . thee may they invoke

23. . . . . hey gave

. . . .

After many lines destroyed, the story recommences in the fourth column.
COLUMN IV.

1. [To Hades the country unseen] I turn myself,

2. I spread like a bird my wings.

3. I descend, I descend to the house of darkness, to the dwelling of the god Irkalla:

4. To the house entering which there is no exit,

5. to the road the course of which never returns:

6. To the house in which the dwellers long for light,

7. the place where dust is their nourishment and their food mud.

8. Its chiefs also are like birds covered with feathers

9. and light is never seen, in darkness they dwell.

10. In the house my friend which I will enter,

11. for me is treasured up a crown;

12. with those wearing crowns who from days of old ruled the earth,

13. to whom the gods Anu and Bel have given terrible names.

14. The food is made carrion, they drink stagnant water.

15. In the house my friend which I will enter,

16. dwell the chiefs and unconquered ones,

17. dwell the bards and great men,

18. dwell the monsters of the deep of the great gods,

19. it is the dwelling of Etana, the dwelling of Ner,

20. . . . . the queen of the lower regions Ninkigal

21. the mistress of the fields the mother of the queen of the lower regions before her submits,

22. and there is not any one that stands against her in her presence.

23. I will approach her and she will see me

24. . . . and she will bring me to her

Here the story is again lost, columns V. and VI. being absent. It is evident that in the third column some one is speaking to Ishtar trying to persuade her not to descend to Hades, while in the fourth column the goddess, who is suffering all the pangs of jealousy and hate, revels in the dark details of the description of the lower regions, and declares her determination to go there.

There can be no doubt that this part of the legend is closely connected with the beautiful story of the Descent of Ishtar into Hades on a tablet which I published in the "Daily Telegraph," in fact I think that tablet to have been an extract from this part of the Izdubar legends, and it so closely connects itself with the story here that I give it as part of the sequel to this tablet.

The descent of Ishtar into Hades from K.

1. To Hades the land of . . . .

2. Ishtar daughter of Sin (the moon) her ear inclined;

3. inclined also the daughter of Sin her ear,

4. to the house of darkness the dwelling of the god Irkalla,

5. to the house entering which there is no exit,

6. to the road the course of which never returns,

7. to the house which on entering it they long for light,

8. the place where dust is their nourishment and their food mud.

9. Light is never seen in darkness they dwell,

10. its chiefs also are like birds covered with feathers,

11. over the door and bolts is scattered dust.

12. Ishtar on her arrival at the gate of Hades,

13. to the keeper of the gate a command she called:

14. Keeper of the waters open thy gate,

15. open thy gate that I may enter.

16. If thou openest not the gate and I am not admitted;

17. I will strike the door and the door posts I will shatter,

18. I will strike the hinges and I will burst open the doors;

19. I will raise up the dead devourers of the living,

20. over the living the dead shall triumph.

21. The keeper his mouth opened and spake,

22. and called to the princess Ishtar:

23. Stay lady do not do this,

24. let me go and thy speech repeat to the queen Ninkigal.

25. The keeper entered and called to Ninkigal:

26. this water thy sister Ishtar . . . .

27 of the great vaults . . . .

28. Ninkigal on her hearing this

29. like the cutting off of . . . .

30. like the bite of an insect it . . . .

31. Will her heart support it, will her spirit uphold it;

32. this water I with . . . .

33. like food eaten like jugs of water drank . . .

34. Let her mourn for the husbands who forsake their wives.

35. Let her mourn for the wives who from the bosom of their husbands depart.

36. for the children who miscarry let her mourn, who are not born in their proper time.

37. Go keeper open thy gate

38. and enclose her like former visitors.

39. The keeper went and opened his gate,

40. on entering lady may the city of Cutha be . .

41. the palace of Hades is rejoicing at thy presence.

42. The first gate he passed her through and drew her in, and he took away the great crown of her head.

43. Why keeper hast thou taken away the great crown of my head.

44. On Entering lady, the goddess of the lower regions does thus with her visitors.

45. The second gate he passed her through and drew her in, and he took away the earrings of her ears.

46. Why keeper hast thou taken away the earrings of my ears.

47. On entering Lady, the goddess of the lower regions does thus with her visitors.

48. The third gate he passed her through and drew her in, and he took away the necklace of her neck.

49. Why keeper hast thou taken away the necklace of my neck.

50. On entering Lady, the goddess of the lower regions does thus with her visitors.

51. The fourth gate he passed her through and drew her in, and he took away the ornaments of her breast.

52. Why keeper hast thou taken away the ornaments of my breast.

53. On entering Lady, the goddess of the lower regions does thus with her visitors.

54. The fifth gate he passed her through and drew her in, and he took away the binding girdle of her waist.

55. Why keeper hast thou taken away the binding girdle of my waist.

56. On entering lady, the goddess of the lower regions does thus with her visitors.

57. The sixth gate he passed her through and drew her in, and he took away the bracelets of her hands and her feet.

58. Why keeper hast thou taken away the bracelets of my hands and my feet.

59. On entering lady, the goddess of the lower regions does thus with her visitors.

60. The seventh gate he passed her through and drew her in, and he took away the covering cloak of her body.

61. Why keeper hast thou taken away the covering cloak of my body.

62. On entering lady, the goddess of the lower regions does thus with her visitors.

63. When a long time Ishtar to Hades had descended;

64. Ninkigal saw her and at her presence was angry,

65. Ishtar did not consider and at her she swore.

66. Ninkigal her mouth opened and spake,

67. to Simtar her attendant a command she called:

68. Go Simtar [take Ishtar from] me and

69. take her out to . . . . Ishtar

70. diseased eyes strike her with,

71. diseased side strike her with,

72. diseased feet strike her with,

73. diseased heart strike her with,

74. diseased head strike her with,

75. to her the whole of her [strike with disease].

76. After Ishtar the lady [to Hades had descended],

77. with the cow the bull would not unite, and the ass the female ass would not approach;

78. and the female slave would not approach the vicinity of the master.

79. The master ceased in his command,

80. the female slave ceased in her gift.

COLUMN II.

1. Papsukul the attendant of the gods, set his face against them

2. turned . . . . full . . . .

3. Samas (the sun) went and in the presence of his father he wept,

4. into the presence of Hea the king he went in tears:

5. Ishtar to the lower regions has descended, she has not returned.

6. When a long time Ishtar to Hades had descended,

7. with the cow the bull would not unite, and the ass the female ass would not approach;

8. and the female slave would not approach the vicinity of the master.

9. The master ceased in his command,

10. the female slave ceased in her gift.

11. Hea in the wisdom of his heart considered,

12. and made Uddusu-namir the sphinx:

13. Go Uddusu-namir towards the gates of Hades set thy face;

14. may the seven gates of Hades be opened at thy presence;

15. may Ninkigal see thee and rejoice at thy arrival.

16. That her heart be satisfied, and her anger be removed;

17. appease her by the names of the great gods.

18. Raise thy heads, on the flowing stream set thy mind,

19. when command over the flowing stream shall be given, the waters in the midst mayest thou drink.

20. Ninkigal on her hearing this,

21. beat her breasts and wrung her hands,

22. she turned at this and comfort would not take:

23. go Uddusu-namir may the great jailor keep thee,

24. May food of the refuse of the city be thy food,

25. May the drains of the city be thy drink,

26. May the shadow of the dungeon be thy resting place,

27. May a slab of stone be thy seat

28. May bondage and want strike thy refuge

29. Ninkigal her mouth opened and spake,

30. to Simtar her attendant a command she called:

31. Go Simtar strike the palace of judgment,

32. the stone slab press upon with the pa-stone,

33. bring out the spirit, and seat it on the golden throne.

34. Over Ishtar pour the water of life and bring her before me.

35. Simtar went, he struck the palace of judgment,

36. the stone slab he pressed upon with the pa-stone,

37. he brought out the spirit and seated it on the golden throne.

38. On Ishtar he poured the water of life and brought her.

39. The first gate he passed her out of, and he restored to her the covering cloak of her body.

40. The second gate he passed her out of, and he restored to her the bracelets of her hands and her feet.

41. The third gate he passed her out of, and he restored to her the binding girdle of her waist.

42. The fourth gate he passed her out of, and he restored to her the ornaments of her breast.

43. The fifth gate he passed her out of, and he restored to her the necklace of her neck.

44. The sixth gate he passed her out of, and he restored to her the earrings of her ears.

45. The seventh gate he passed her out of, and he restored to her the great crown of her head.

46. When her freedom she would not grant to thee to her also turn,

47. to Dumuzi the husband of her youth;

48. beautiful waters pour out beautiful boxes . . . .

49. in splendid clothing dress him, bracelets? of jewels place . . . .

50. May Samhat appease her grief,

51. and Belele give to her comfort.

52. Precious stones like eyes are not . . . .

53. her brother was slain? . . . . she struck, Belele gave her comfort.

54. Precious stones like birds' eyes are not better than thee,

55. my only brother thou didst never wrong me

56. In the day that Dumuzi adorned me, with rings of rubies, with bracelets of emeralds, with him adorned me,

57. with him adorned me, men mourners and women mourners,

58. on a bier may they raise, and gashes? may they cut?

This remarkable text shows Ishtar fulfilling her threat and descending to Hades, but it does not appear that she accomplished her vengeance against Izdubar yet.

At the opening of the sixth tablet we have the final scene of the contest with Humbaba. Izdubar, after slaying. Humbaba, takes the crown from the head of the monarch and places it on his own head, thus signifying that he assumed the empire. There were, as we are informed in several places, kings, lords, and princes, merely local rulers, but these generally submitted to the greatest power; and just as they had bowed to Humbaba, so they were ready now to submit to Izdubar. The kingdom promised to Izdubar when he started to encounter Humbaba now became his by right of superior force, and he entered the halls of the palace of Erech and feasted with his heroes.

We now come to a curious part of the story, the romance of Izdubar and Ishtar. One of the strange and dark features of the Babylonian religion was the Ishtar or Venus worship, which was an adoration of the reproductive power of nature, accompanied by ceremonies which were a reproach to the country. The city of Erech, originally a seat of the worship of Anu, was now one of the foremost cities in this Ishtar worship. Certainly Ishtar is represented in the legends as living at the time, and as being the widow of Dumuzi, the ruler of Erech, and it is possible there may have been some basis for the story in a tradition of some dissolute queen whose favour Izdubar refused; but we have to remember that these Izdubar legends were not intended for history, but for historical romance, and the whole story of Ishtar may be only introduced to show the hero's opposition to this worship, or to make an attack upon the superstition by quoting Izdubar's supposed defiance of the goddess.

The thirteenth to sixteenth lines of the first column appear to mark out the ultimate boundaries of the empire of Izdubar, and the limits mark somewhere about the extent assigned to the kingdom of Nimrod by tradition. The northern boundary was Bitani by the Armenian mountains, the eastern boundary the mountain ranges which separated Assyria and Babylonia from Media, and the south was the Persian Gulf, beyond which nothing was known, and the Arabian desert, which also bounded part of the west. On the western boundary his dominions stretched along the region of the Euphrates, perhaps to Orfa, a city which has still traditions of Nimrod.

In the course of the answer Izdubar gives to Ishtar, he calls to mind the various amours of Ishtar, and I cannot avoid the impression that the author has here typified the universal power of love, extending over high and low, men and animals.

The subsequent lines show Ishtar obtaining from her father the creation of a bull called "the divine bull;" this animal I have supposed to be the winged bull so often depicted on Assyrian sculpture, but I am now inclined to think that this bull is represented without wings. The struggle with a bull, represented on the Babylonian cylinder, figured here, and numerous similar representations, seem to refer to this incident. There is no struggle with a winged bull on the Izdubar cylinders.

It would appear from the broken fragments of column IV. that Heabani laid hold of the bull by the head and tail while Izdubar killed it, and Heabani in the engraving is represented holding the bull by its head and tail.

At the close of the sixth tablet the story is again lost, only portions of the third and fourth columns of the next tablet being preserved, but light is thrown on this portion of the narrative by the remarkable tablet describing the descent of Ishtar into Hades. I think it probable that this tablet was in great part an extract from the seventh tablet of the Izdubar legends.

The tablet with the descent of Ishtar into Hades was first noticed by Mr. Fox Talbot in the "Transactions of the Royal Society of Literature," but he was entirely abroad as to the meaning of the words. After this I published a short notice of it in the "North British Review," to clear up some of the difficulties, and it has been subsequently translated by Lenormant and Oppert, and re-translated by Mr. Fox Talbot. These translations and various notices of the Deluge tablets will be found in "Les Premières Civilisations" of Francois Lenormant, Paris, 1874, a small pamphlet on the Descent of Ishtar, by Professor Oppert, and various papers on these subjects by Mr. Fox Talbot, in the "Transactions of the Society of Biblical Archæology," vols. i., ii., and iii., and my own translation in the "Daily Telegraph," August 19, 1873.

The story of the descent of Ishtar into Hades is one of the most beautiful myths in the Assyrian inscriptions; it has, however, received so much attention, and been so fully commented upon by various scholars, that little need be said on the subject here.

It is evident that we are dealing with the same goddess as the Ishtar, daughter of Anu, in the Izdubar legends, although she is here called daughter of Sin (the moon god) .

The description of the region of Hades is most graphic, and vividly portrays the sufferings of the prisoners there; but there are several difficulties in the story, as there is no indication in some cases as to who acts or speaks. Uddusu-namir, created by Hea to deliver Ishtar, is described as a composite animal, half bitch and half man, with more than one head, and appears to correspond, in some respects, to the Cerberus of the classics, which had three heads according to some, fifty heads according to others.

The latter part of the tablet is obscure, and appears to refer to the custom of lamenting for Dumuzi or Tammuz.

CHAPTER XV: ILLNESS AND WANDERINGS OF IZDUBAR.

Heabani and the trees.—Illness of Izdubar.—Death of Heabani.—
Journey of Izdubar.—His dream.—Scorpion men.—The Desert of
Mas.—The paradise.—Siduri and Sabitu.—Urhamsi.—Water of
death.—Ragmu.—The conversation.—Hasisadra.

OF the three tablets in this section, the first one is very uncertain, and is
put together from two separate sources; the other two are more complete
and satisfactory.

TABLET VIII.

I am uncertain again if I have discovered any of this tablet; I
provisionally place here some fragments of the first, second, third, and
sixth columns of a tablet which may belong to it, but the only fragment
worth translating at present is one I have given in "Assyrian Discoveries,"
p. 176. In some portions of these fragments there are references, as I have
there stated, to the story of Humbaba, but as the fragment appears to refer
to the illness of Izdubar I think it belongs here.

COLUMN I.

1. to his friend . . . .
2 and 3 . . . .
4. thy name . . .
5. . . . .
6. his speech he made . . . .
7. Izdubar my father . . . .
8. Izdubar . . . .
9. . . . .
10. joined . . .

---

11. Heabani his mouth opened and spake and
12. said to . . . .
13. I join him . . . .
14. in the . . . .
15. the door . . . .
16. of. . . .

17 and 18. . . .

19. in. . . .

20. Heabani . . . . carried . . .

21. with the door . . . . thy . . .

22. the door on its sides does not . . .

23. it has not aroused her hearing . . .

24. for twenty kaspu (140 miles) it is raised . . .

25. and the pine tree a bush I see . . .

26. there is not another like thy tree . . .

27. Six gars (120 feet) is thy height, two gars (40 feet) is thy breadth . . . .

28. thy circuit, thy contents, thy mass . . .

29. thy make which is in thee in the city of Nipur . . . .

30. I know thy entrance like this . . .

31. and this is good . . .

32. for I have his face, for I . . .

33. I fill . . . .

34. . . . . .

35. for he took . . .

36. the pine tree, the cedar, . . .

37. in its cover . . .

38. thou also . . . .

39. may take . . .

40. in the collection of everything . . .

41. a great destruction . . .

42. the whole of the trees . . .

43. in thy land Izmanubani . . .

44. thy bush? is not strong . . .

45. thy shadow is not great . . .

46. and thy smell is not agreeable . . .

---

47. The Izmanubani tree was angry . . .

48. made a likeness?

49. like the tree . . .

. . . . . .

The second, third, fourth and fifth columns appear to be entirely absent, the inscription reappearing on a fragment of the sixth column.

COLUMN II.

(Many lines lost.)

1. The dream which I saw . . . .
2. . . . . made? the mountain . . . .
3. he struck . . . .
4. They like *nimgi* struck . . . .
5. brought? forth in the vicinity . . . .
6. He said to his friend Heabani the dream . . .
7. . . . . good omen of the dream . . . .
8. the dream was deceptive . . . .
9. all the mountain which thou didst see . . . .
10. when we captured Humbaba and we . . . .
11. . . . . of his helpers to thy . . . .
12. in the storm to . . . .

---

13. For twenty kaspu he journeyed a stage
14. at thirty kaspu he made a halt?
15. in the presence of Shamas he dug out a pit . . . .
16. Izdubar ascended to over . . . .
17. by the side of his house he approached . . . .
18. the mountain was subdued, the dream . . . .
19. he made it and . . . .

COLUMN III.

1. The mountain was subdued, the dream . . . .
2. he made it and . . . .
3. . . . . turban? . . . .
4. he cast him down and . . . .
5. the mountain like corn of the field . . . .
6. Izdubar at the destruction set up . . . .
7. Anatu the injurer of men upon him struck,
8. and in the midst of his limbs he died.
9. He spake and said to his friend:
10. Friend thou dost not ask me why I am naked,
11. thou dost not inquire of me why I am spoiled,
12. God will not depart, why do my limbs burn.
13. Friend I saw a third dream,
14. and the dream which I saw entirely disappeared,
15. He invoked the god of the earth and desired death.
16. A storm came out of the darkness,
17. the lightning struck and kindled a fire,

18. and came out the shadow of death.

19. It disappeared, the fire sank,

20. he struck it and it turned to a palm tree,

21. . . . and in the desert thy lord was proceeding.

22. And Heabani the dream considered and said to Izdubar.

The fourth and fifth columns of this tablet are lost. This part of the legend appears to refer to the illness of Izdubar.

COLUMN VI.

1. My friend . . . the dream which is not . . .

2. the day he dreamed the dream, the end . . .

3. Heabani lay down also one day . . .

4. which Heabani in that evening . . .

5. the third day and the fourth day which . . .

6. the fifth, sixth, seventh, eighth, ninth . . .

7. when Heabani was troubled . . .

8. the eleventh and twelfth . . .

9. Heabani in that evening . . .

10. Izdubar asked also . . .

11. is my friend hostile to me . . .

12. then in the midst of fight . . .

13. I turn to battle and . . .

14. the friend who in battle . . .

15. I in . . . . . .

. . . .

It must here be noted that my grounds for making this the eighth tablet are extremely doubtful, it is possible that the fragments are of different tablets; but they fill up an evident blank in the story here, and I have inserted them pending further discoveries as to their true position.

In the first column Heabani appears to be addressing certain trees, and they are supposed to have the power of hearing and answering him. Heabani praises one tree and sneers at another, but from the mutilation of the text it does not appear why he acts so. I conjecture he was seeking a charm to open the door he mentions, and that according to the story this charm was known to the trees. The fragment of the sixth column shows Heabani unable to interpret a dream, while Izdubar asks his friend to fight.

After this happened the violent death of Heabani, which added to the misfortunes of Izdubar; but no fragment of this part of the story is preserved.

TABLET IX.

This tablet is in a somewhat better state than the others, and all the narrative is clearer from this point, not a single column of the inscription being entirely lost. The ninth tablet commences with the sorrow of Izdubar at the death of Heabani.

COLUMN I.

1. Izdubar over Heabani his seer
2. bitterly lamented, and lay down on the ground.
3. I had no judgment like Heabani;
4. Weakness entered into my soul;
5. death I feared, and lay down on the ground.
6. For the advice of Hasisadra, son of Ubaratutu
7. The road I was taking, and joyfully I went,
8. to the neighbourhood of the mountains I took at night.
9. a dream I saw, and I feared.
10. I bowed on my face, and to Sin (the moon god) I prayed;
11. and into the presence of the gods came my supplication;
12. and they sent peace unto me.
13. . . . . . . dream.
14. . . . . . Sin, erred in life.
15. precious stones . . . to his hand.
16. were bound to his girdle
17. like the time . . . their . . . he struck
18. he struck . . . . fruit? he broke
19. and. . . .
20. he threw . . . .
21. he was guarded . . .
22. the former name . . . .
23. the new name . . . .
24. he carried . . . .
25. to. . . .

(About six lines lost here.)

The second column shows Izdubar in some fabulous region, whither he has wandered in search of Hasisadra. Here he sees composite monsters with their feet resting in hell, and their heads reaching heaven. These

151

beings are supposed to guide and direct the sun at its rising and setting. This passage is as follows:—

COLUMN II.

1. Of the country hearing him . . . .

2. To the mountains of Mas in his course . . . .

3. who each day guard the rising sun.

4. Their crown was at the lattice of heaven,

5. under hell their feet were placed.

6. The scorpion-man guarded the gate,

7. burning with terribleness, their appearance was like death,

8. the might of his fear shook the forests.

9. At the rising of the sun and the setting of the sun, they guarded the sun.

10. Izdubar saw them and fear and terror came into his face.

11. Summoning his resolution he approached before them.

12. The scorpion-man of his female asked:

13. Who comes to us with the affliction of god on his body

14. To the scorpion-man his female answered:

15. The work of god is laid upon the man,

16. The scorpion-man of the hero asked,

17. . . . . . of the gods the word he said:

18. . . . . . distant road

19. . . . . . come to my presence

20. . . . . . of which the passage is difficult.

The rest of this column is lost. In it Izdubar converses with the monsters and where the third column begins he is telling them his purpose, to seek Hasisadra.

COLUMN III.

(1 and 2 lost.)

3. He Hasisadra my father . . . . .

4. who is established in the assembly of the gods

5. death and life [are known to him]

6. The monster opened his mouth and spake

7. and said to Izdubar

8. Do it not Izdubar . . . .

9. of the country . . . .

10. for twelve kaspu (84 miles) [is the journey]

11. which is completely covered with sand, and there is not a cultivated field,

12. to the rising sun . . . .

13. to the setting sun . . . .

14. to the setting sun . . . .

15. he brought out . . . .

In this mutilated passage, the monster describes the journey to be taken by Izdubar; there are now many lines wanting, until we come to the fourth column.

COLUMN IV.

1. in prayer . . . .

2. again thou . . . .

3. the monster . . . .

4. Izdubar . . . .

5. go Izdubar . . . .

6. lands of Mas . . . .

7. the road of the sun . . . .

8. 1 kaspu he went . . . .

9. which was completely covered with sand, and there was not a cultivated field,

10. he was not able to look behind him.

11. 2 kaspu he went . . . .

This is the bottom of the fourth column; there are five lines lost at the top of the fifth column, and then the narrative reopens; the text is, however, mutilated and doubtful.

COLUMN V.

6. 4 kaspu he went . . . .

7. which was completely covered with sand, and there was not a cultivated field,

8. he was not able to look behind him.

9. 5 kaspu he went . . . .

10. which was completely covered with sand, and there was not a cultivated field,

11. he was not able to look behind him.

12. 6 kaspu he went . . . .

13. which was completely covered with sand, and there was not a cultivated field,

14. he was not able to look behind him.

15. 7 kaspu he went . . . .

16. which was completely covered with sand, and there was not a cultivated field,

17. he was not able to look behind him.

18. 8 kaspu he went . . . . turned? . . . .

19. which was completely covered with sand, and there was not a cultivated field,

20. he was not able to look behind him.

21. 9 kaspu he went . . . . to the north

22. . . . . . his face

23. . . . . . a field

24. . . . . . to look behind him

25. 10 kaspu? he went? . . . . him

26. . . . . meeting

27. . . . . . 4 kaspu

28. . . . . . shadow of the sun

29. . . . . beautiful situation . . . .

30. to the forest of the trees of the gods in appearance it was equal.

31. Emeralds it carried as its fruit,

32. the branches were encircled to the points covered,

33. Ukni stones it carried as shoots?

34. the fruit it carried to the sight were large

Some of the words in this fragment are obscure, but the general meaning is clear. In the next column the wanderings of Izdubar are continued, and he comes to a country near the sea. Fragments of several lines of this column are preserved, but too mutilated to translate with certainty. The fragments are:—

COLUMN VI.

(About six lines lost.)

1. the pine tree . . . .

2. its nest of stone . . . . ukni stone?

3. not striking the sea . . . . jet stones

4. like worms? and caterpillars . . . . gugmi

5. a bustard it caught? beautiful

6. jet stone, ka stone . . . . the goddess Ishtar

7. . . . . . he carried

8. like . . . . *asgege*

9. which . . . . the sea

10. was . . . . may he raise

11. Izdubar [saw this] in his travelling

12. and he carried . . . . that

This tablet brings Izdubar to the region of the sea-coast, but his way is then barred by two women, one named Siduri, and the other Sabitu. His further adventures are given on the tenth tablet, which opens:

TABLET X.

1. Siduri and Sabitu who in the land beside the sea dwelt

2. dwelt also . . . .

3. making a dwelling, making . . . .

4. covered with stripes of affliction in . . . .

5. Izdubar struck with disease . . . .

6. illness covering his . . . .

7. having the brand of the gods on his . . . .

8. there was shame of face on . . . .

9. to go on the distant path his face was set.

10. Sabitu afar off pondered,

11. spake within her heart, and a resolution made.

12. Within herself also she considered:

13. What is this message

14. There is no one upright in . . . .

15. And Sabitu saw him and shut her place?

16. her gate she shut, and shut her place?

17. And he Izdubar having ears heard her

18. he struck his hands and made . . . .

---

19. Izdubar to her also said to Sabitu:

20. Sabitu why dost thou shut thy place?

21. thy gate thou closest . . . .

22. I will strike the . . . .

The rest of this column is lost, but I am able to say it described the meeting of Izdubar with a boatman named Urhamsi, and they commence together a journey by water in a boat on the second column. Very little of this column is preserved; I give two fragments only here.

COLUMN II.

1. Urhamsi to him also said to Izdubar

2. Why should I curse thee . . . .

---

3. and thy heart is tried . . . .

4. there is shame of face on . . . .

5. thou goest on the distant path . . . .

6. . . . . burning and affliction . . . .

7. . . . . thus thou . . . .

8. Izdubar to him also said to Urhamsi

9. . . . . . my hand has not . . . .

10. . . . . . my heart is not . . . .

11. . . . . . shame of face on . . . .

Here again there are many wanting lines, and then we have some fragments of the bottom of the column.

1. . . . . . said to Izdubar

2. . . . . . and his lower part

3. . . . . . the ship

4. . . . . . of death

5. . . . . . wide

6. . . . . . ends

7. . . . . . to the river

8. . . . . . ship

9. . . . . . in the vicinity

10. . . . . boatman

11. . . . . . he burned

12. . . . . . to thee

Here there are many lines lost, then recommencing the story proceeds on the third column.

COLUMN III.

1. the friend whom I loved . . . .

2. I am not like him . . . .

---

3. Izdubar to him also said to Ur-hamsi

4. Again Ur-hamsi why . . . .

5. what brings (matters) to me if it . . . .

6. if carried to cross the sea, if not carried [to cross the sea]

---

7. Ur-hamsi to him also said to Izdubar

8. Thy hand Izdubar ceases . . . .

9. thou hidest in the place of the stones thou . . .

10. in the place of the stones hidden and they . . .

11. Take Izdubar the axe in thy hand . . . .

12. go down to the forest and a spear of five gar . . .

13. capture and make a burden of it, and carry it . . .

14. Izdubar on his hearing this,

15. took the axe in his hand . . . .

16. he went down to the forest and a spear of five gar. . . .

17. he took and made a burden of it, and carried it [to the ship]

18. Izdubar and Urhamsi rode in the ship

19. the ship the waves took and they . . . .

20. a journey of one month and fifteen days. On the third day in their course

21. took Urhamsi the waters of death . . . .

COLUMN IV.

1. Urhamsi to him also said to Izdubar

2. the tablets? Izdubar . . .

3. Let not the waters of death enclose thy hand. . . .

4. the second time, the third time, and the fourth time Izdubar was lifting the spear . . . .

5. the fifth, sixth, and seventh time Izdubar was lifting the spear . . . .

6. the eighth, ninth, and tenth time Izdubar was lifting the spear . . . .

7. the eleventh and twelfth time, Izdubar was lifting the spear . . . .

8. on the one hundred and twentieth time Izdubar finished the spear

9. and he broke his girdle to . . . .

10. Izdubar seized the . . . .

11. on, his wings a cord he . . . .

12. Hasisadra afar off pondered,

13. spake within his heart and a resolution made.

14. Within himself also he considered:

15. Why is the ship still hidden

16. is not ended the voyage . . . .

17. the man is not come to me and . . . .

18. I wonder he is not . . . . .

19. I wonder he is not . . . .

20. I wonder . . . .

Here there is a blank, the extent of which is uncertain, and where the narrative recommences it is on a small fragment of the third and fourth column of another copy. It appears that the lost lines record the meeting between Izdubar and a person named Ragmu-seri-ina-namari. I have conjectured that this individual was the wife of Hasisadra or Noah; but there is no ground for this opinion; it is possible that this individual was the gatekeeper or guard, by whom Izdubar had to pass in going to reach Hasisadra.

It is curious that, whenever Izdubar speaks to this being, the name Ragmua is used, while, whenever Izdubar is spoken to, the full name Ragmu-seri-ina-namari occurs. Where the story re-opens Izdubar is informing Ragmu of his first connection with Heabani and his offers to him when he desired him to come to Erech.

COLUMN III. (fragment).

1. for my friend . . . .

2. free thee . . . .

3. weapon . . . .

4. bright star . . . .

COLUMN IV. (fragment).

1. On a beautiful couch I will seat thee,

2. I will cause thee to sit on a comfortable seat on the left,

3. the kings of the earth shall kiss thy feet.

4. I will enrich thee and the men of Erech I will make silent before thee,

5. and I after thee will take all . . . .

6. I will clothe thy body in raiment and . . . .

---

7. Ragmu-seri-ina-namari on his hearing this

8. his fetters loosed . . . .

The speech of Ragmu to Izdubar and the rest of the column are lost, the narrative recommencing on Column V. with another speech of Izdubar.

COLUMN V. (fragment).

1. . . . . to me

2. . . . . my . . . I wept

3. . . . . bitterly I spoke

4. . . . . my hand

5. . . . . ascended to me

6. . . . . to me

---

7. . . . . leopard of the desert

COLUMN V.

1. Izdubar opened his mouth and said to Ragmu

2. . . . . my presence?

3. . . . . not strong

4. . . . . my face

5. . . . . lay down in the field,

6. . . . . of the mountain, the leopard of the field,

7. Heabani my friend . . . . the same.

8. No one else was with us, we ascended the mountain.

9. We took it and the city we destroyed.

10. We conquered also Humbaba who in the forest of pine trees dwelt.

11. Again why did his fingers lay hold to slay the lions.

12. Thou wouldst have feared and thou wouldst not have . . all the difficulty.

13. And he did not succeed in slaying the same

14. his heart failed, and he did not strike . . . . over him I wept,

15. he covered also my friend like a corpse in a grave,

16. like a lion? he tore? him

17. like a lioness? placed . . . . field

18. he was cast down to the face of the earth

19. he broke? and destroyed his defence? . . . .

20. he was cut off and given to pour out? . . . .

---

21. Ragmu-seri-ina-namari on hearing this

Here the record is again mutilated, Izdubar further informs Ragmu what he did in conjunction with Heabani. Where the story reopens on Column VI. Izdubar relates part of their adventure with Humbaba.

COLUMN VI.

1. . . . . taking

2. . . . . to thee

3. . . . . thou art great

4. . . . . all the account

---

5. . . . . forest of pine trees

6. . . . . went night and day

7. . . . . the extent of Erech Suburi

8. . . . . he approached after us

9. . . . . he opened the land of forests

10. . . . . we ascended

11. . . . . in the midst like thy mother

12. . . . . cedar and pine trees

13. . . . . with our strength

14. . . . . silent

15. . . . . he of the field

16. . . . . by her side

17. . . . . the Euphrates

Here again our narrative is lost, and where we again meet the story Izdubar has spoken to Hasisadra and is receiving his answer.

1. I was angry . . . .

2. Whenever a house was built, whenever a treasure was collected

3. Whenever brothers fixed . . . .

4. Whenever hatred is in . . . .

5. Whenever the river makes a great flood.

p. 261

6. Whenever reviling within the mouth . . . .

7. the face that bowed before Shamas

8. from of old was not . . . .

9. Spoiling and death together exist

10. of death the image has not been seen.

11. The man or servant on approaching death,

12. the spirit of the great gods takes his hand.

13. The goddess Mamitu maker of fate, to them their fate brings,

14. she has fixed death and life;

15. of death the day is not known.

This statement of Hasisadra closes the tenth tablet and leads to the next question of Izdubar and its answer, which included the story of the Flood.

The present division of the legends has its own peculiar difficulties; in the first place it does not appear how Heabani was killed. My original idea, that he was killed by the poisonous insect *tambukku*, I find to be incorrect, and it now appears most likely either that he was killed in a quarrel with Izdubar or that he fell in an attempt to slay a lion.

In the ninth tablet I am able to make a correction to my former translation; I find the monsters seen by Izdubar were composite beings, half scorpions, half men. The word for scorpion has been some time ago discovered by Professor Oppert, and I find it occurs in the description of these beings; also on a fragment of a tablet which I found at Kouyunjik the star of the scorpion is said to belong to the eighth month, in which, of course, it should naturally appear.

This assists in explaining a curious tablet printed in "Cuneiform Inscriptions," vol. iii. p. 52, No. 1, which has been misunderstood. This tablet speaks of the appearance of comets, one of which has a tail "like a lizard (or creeping thing) and a scorpion."

The land of Mas or desert of Mas over which Izdubar travels in this tablet is the desert on the west of the Euphrates; on the sixth column the fragments appear to refer to some bird with magnificent feathers like precious stones, seen by Izdubar on his journey.

I have altered my translation of the passage in pp. 255, 256, which I now believe to relate that Izdubar at the direction of Urhamsi made a spear from one of the trees of the forest before going across the waters of death which separated the abode of Hasisadra from the world of mortals. I do not, however, understand the passage, as from the mutilated condition of the inscription it does not appear what he attacked with it.

CHAPTER XVI: THE STORY OF THE FLOOD AND CONCLUSION.

Eleventh tablet.—The gods.—Sin of the world.—Command to build the ark.—Its contents.—The building.—The Flood.—Destruction of people.—Fear of the gods.—End of Deluge.—Nizir.—Resting of ark.—The birds.—The descent from the ark.—The sacrifice.—Speeches of gods.—Translation of Hasisadra.—Cure of Izdubar.—His return.—Lament over Heabani.—Resurrection of Heabani.—Burial of warrior.—Comparison with Genesis.—Syrian nation.—Connection of legends.—Points of contact.—Duration of deluge.—Mount of descent—Ten generations.—Early cities.—Age of Izdubar.

THE eleventh tablet of the Izdubar series is the one which first attracted attention, and certainly the most important on account of its containing the story of the Flood. This tablet is the most perfect in the series, scarcely any line being entirely lost.

TABLET XI.

COLUMN I.

1. Izdubar after this manner also said to Hasisadra afar off:

2. I consider the matter,

3. why thou repeatest not to me from thee,

4. and thou repeatest not to me from thee,

5. thy ceasing my heart to make war

6. presses? of thee, I come up after thee,

7. . . . . how thou hast done, and in the assembly of the gods alive thou art placed.

---

8. Hasisadra after this manner also said to Izdubar:

9. Be revealed to thee Izdubar the concealed story,

10. and the judgment of the gods be related to thee,

11. The city Surippak the city where thou standest not . . . . placed,

12. that city is ancient . . . . the gods within it

13. . . . . . . their servant, the great gods

14. . . . . . . the god Anu,

15. . . . . . . the god Bel,

16. . . . . . . the god Ninip,
17. and the god . . . . lord of Hades;
18. their will he revealed in the midst . . . . and
19. I his will was hearing and he spake to me:
20. Surippakite son of Ubaratutu
21. . . . . . make a ship after this . . . .
22. . . . . . I destroy? the sinner and life . . . .
23. . . . . . cause to go in? the seed of life all of it to the midst of the ship.
24. The ship which thou shalt make,
25. 600? cubits shall be the measure of its length, and
26. 60? cubits the amount of its breadth and its height.
27. . . . into the deep launch it.
28. I perceived and said to Hea my lord:
29. The ship making which thou commandest me,
30. when I shall have made,
31. young and old will deride me.
32. Hea opened his mouth and spake and said to me his servant:
33. . . . . thou shalt say unto them,
34. . . . . . . he has turned from me and
35. . . . . fixed over me
36. . . . . . like caves . . . .
37. . . . above and below
38. . . . closed the ship . . .
39. . . . the flood which I will send to you,
40. into it enter and the door of the ship turn.
41. Into the midst of it thy grain, thy furniture, and thy goods,
42. thy wealth, thy woman servants, thy female slaves, and the young men,
43. the beasts of the field, the animals of the field all, I will gather and
44. I will send to thee, and they shall be enclosed in thy door.

---

45. Adrahasis his mouth opened and spake, and
46. said to Hea his lord:
47. Any one the ship will not make . . .
48. on the earth fixed . . . .
49. . . . . I may see also the ship . . . .
50. . . . . on the ground the ship . . . .
51. the ship making which thou commandest me . .

52. which in . . . .

COLUMN II.

1. strong . . . .

2. on the fifth day . . . . it

3. in its circuit 14 measures . . . its frame.

4. 14 measures it measured . . . over it.

5. I placed its roof, it . . . . I enclosed it.

6. I rode in it on the sixth time; I examined its exterior on the seventh time;

7. its interior I examined on the eighth time.

8. Planks against the waters within it I placed.

9. I saw rents and the wanting parts I added.

10. 3 measures of bitumen I poured over the outside.

11. 3 measures of bitumen I poured over the inside.

12. 3 . . . men carrying its baskets, they constructed boxes

13. I placed in the boxes the offering they sacrificed.

14. Two measures of boxes I had distributed to the boatmen.

15. To . . . . were sacrificed oxen

16. . . . . dust and

17. . . . . wine in receptacle of goats 18. I collected like the waters of a river, also

19. food like the dust of the earth also

20. I collected in boxes with my hand I placed.

21. . . . . Shamas . . . . material of the ship completed.

22. . . . . strong and

23. the reed oars of the ship I caused to bring above and below.

24. . . . . they went in two-thirds of it.

---

25. All I possessed the strength of it, all I possessed the strength of it silver,

26. all I possessed the strength of it gold,

27. all I possessed the strength of it the seed of life, the whole

28. I caused to go up into the ship; all my male servants and my female servants,

29. the beast of the field, the animal of the field, the sons of the people all of' them, I caused to go up.

30. A flood Shamas made and

31. he spake saying in the night: I will cause it to rain heavily,

32. enter to the midst of the ship and shut thy door.

33. that flood happened, of which

34. he spake saying in the night: I will cause it to rain (or it will rain) from heaven heavily.

35. In the day I celebrated his festival

36. the day of watching fear I had.

37. I entered to the midst of the ship and shut my door.

38. To close the ship to Buzur-sadirabi the boatman

39. the palace I gave with its goods.

---

40. Ragmu-seri-ina-namari

41. arose, from the horizon of heaven extending and wide.

42. Vul in the midst of it thundered, and

43. Nebo and Saru went in front,

44. the throne bearers went over mountains and plains,

45. the destroyer Nergal overturned,

46. Ninip went in front and cast down,

47. the spirits carried destruction,

48. in their glory they swept the earth;

49. of Vul the flood reached to heaven.

50. The bright earth to a waste was turned,

COLUMN III.

1. the surface of the earth like . . . . it swept,

2. it destroyed all life from the face of the earth. . . . .

3. the strong deluge over the people, reached to heaven.

4. Brother saw not his brother, they did not know the people. In heaven

5. the gods feared the tempest and

6. sought refuge; they ascended to the heaven of Anu.

7. The gods like dogs fixed in droves prostrate.

8. Spake Ishtar like a child,

9. uttered Rubat her speech:

10. All to corruption are turned and

11. then I in the presence of the gods prophesied evil.

12. As I prophesied in the presence of the gods evil,

13. to evil were devoted all my people and I prophesied

14. thus: I have begotten my people and

15. like the young of the fishes they fill the sea.

16. The gods concerning the spirits were weeping with her,

17. the gods in seats seated in lamentation,

18. covered were their lips for the coming evil.

19. Six days and nights

20. passed, the wind, deluge, and storm, overwhelmed.

21. On the seventh day in its course was calmed the storm, and all the deluge

22. which had destroyed like an earthquake,

23. quieted. The sea he caused to dry, and the wind and deluge ended.

24. I perceived the sea making a tossing;

25. and the whole of mankind turned to corruption,

26. like reeds the corpses floated.

27. I opened the window, and the light broke over my face,

28. it passed. I sat down and wept,

29. over my face flowed my tears.

30. I perceived the shore at the boundary of the sea,

31. for twelve measures the land rose.

32. To the country of Nizir went the ship;

33. the mountain of Nizir stopped the ship, and to pass over it it was not able.

34. The first day, and the second day, the mountain of Nizir the same.

35. The third day, and the fourth day, the mountain of Nizir the same.

36. The fifth, and sixth, the mountain of Nizir the same.

37. On the seventh day in the course of it

---

38. I sent forth a dove and it left. The dove went and turned, and

39. a resting-place it did not find, and it returned.

40. I sent forth a swallow and it left. The swallow went and turned, and

41. a resting-place it did not find, and it returned.

42. I sent forth a raven and it left.

43. The raven went, and the decrease of the water it saw, and

44. it did eat, it swam, and wandered away, and did not return.

45. I sent the animals forth to the four winds, I poured out a libation,

46. I built an altar on the peak of the mountain,

47. by sevens herbs I cut,

48. at the bottom of them I placed reeds, pines, and simgar.

49. The gods collected at its savour, the gods collected at its good savour;

50. the gods like flies over the sacrifice gathered.

51. From of old also Rubat in her course

52. The great brightness of Anu had created. When the glory

53. of those gods on the charm round my neck I would not leave;

COLUMN IV.

1. in those days I desired that for ever I might not leave them.

2. May the gods come to my altar,

3. may Elu not come to my altar,

4. for he did not consider and had made a deluge,

5. and my people he had consigned to the deep.

6. From of old also Elu in his course

7. saw the ship, and went Elu with anger filled to the gods and spirits:

8. Let not any one come out alive, let not a man be saved from the deep,

9. Ninip his mouth opened, and spake and said to the warrior Elu

10. Who then will ask Hea, the matter he has done?

11. and Hea knew all things.

12. Hea his mouth opened and spake, and said to the warrior Bel:

13. "Thou prince of the gods warrior,

14. when thou art angry a deluge thou makest;

15. the doer of sin did his sin, the doer of evil did his evil.

16. the just prince let him not be cut off, the faithful let him not be destroyed.

17. Instead of thee making a deluge, may lions increase and men be reduced;

18. instead of thee making a deluge, may leopards increase and men be reduced;

19. instead of thee making a deluge, may a famine happen and the country be destroyed;

20. instead of thee making a deluge, may pestilence increase and men be destroyed."

21. I did not peer into the judgment of the gods.

22. Adrahasis a dream they sent, and the judgment of the gods he heard.

23. When his judgment was accomplished, Bel went up to the midst of the ship.

24. He took my hand and raised me up,

25. he caused to raise and to bring my wife to my side;

26. he made a bond, he established in a covenant, and gave this blessing,

27. in the presence of Hasisadra and the people thus:

28. When Hasisadra, and his wife, and the people, to be like the gods are carried away;

29. then shall dwell Hasisadra in a remote place at the mouth of the rivers.

30. They took me, and in a remote place at the mouth of the rivers they seated me.

31. When to thee whom the gods have chosen also,

32. for the health which thou seekest and askest,

33. this be done six days and seven nights,

34. like sitting on the edge of his seat,

35. the way like a storm shall be laid upon him.

36. Hasisadra to her also said to his wife

37. I announce that the chief who grasps at health

38. the way like a storm shall be laid upon him.

39. His wife to him also said to Hasisadra afar off:

40. clothe him, and let the man be sent away;

41. the road that he came may he return in peace,

42. the great gate open and may he return to his country.

43. Hasisadra to her also said to his wife:

44. The cry of a man alarms thee,

45. this do his *kurummat* place on his head.

46. And the day when he ascended the side of the ship,

47. she did, his *kurummat* she placed on his head.

48. And the day when he ascended the side of the ship,

49. first the *sabusat* of his *kurummat*,

50. second the *mussukat*, third the *radbat*, fourth she opened his *zikaman*,

51. fifth the cloak she placed, sixth the *bassat*,

COLUMN V.

1. seventh in a mantle she clothed him and let the man go free.

2. Izdubar to him also said to Hasisadra afar off:

3. In this way thou vast compassionate over me,

4. joyfully thou hast made me, and thou hast restored me.

5. Hasisadra to him also said to Izdubar.

6. . . . . . . thy *kurummit*,

7. . . . . . . separated thee,

8. . . . . . . thy *kurummat*,

9. second the *mussukat*, third the *radbat*,

10. fourth she opened the *zikaman*,

11. fifth the cloak she placed, sixth the *bassat*,

12. seventh in a cloak I have clothed thee and let thee go free.

13. Izdubar to him also said to Hasisadra afar off:

14. . . . . Hasisadra to thee may we not come,

15. . . . . collected

16. . . . . dwelling in death,

17. . . . . his back? dies also.

---

18. Hasisadra to him also said to Urhamsi the boatman:

19. Urhamsi . . . . . . to thee we cross to preserve thee.

20. Who is beside the . . . . . . of support;

21. the man whom thou comest before, disease has filled his body;

22. illness has destroyed the strength of his limbs.

23. carry him Urhamsi, to cleanse take him,

24. his disease in the water to beauty may it turn,

25. may he cast off his illness, and the sea carry it away, may health cover his skin,

26. may it restore the hair of his head,

27. hanging to cover the cloak of his body.

28. That he may go to his country, that he may take his road,

29. the hanging cloak may he not cast off, but alone may he leave.

30. Urhamsi carried him, to cleanse he took him,

31. his disease in the water to beauty turned,

32. he cast off his illness, and the sea carried it away, and health covered his skin,

33. he restored the hair of his head, hanging down to cover the cloak of his body.

34. That he might go to his country, that he might take his road,

35. the hanging cloak he did not cast off, but alone he left.

36. Izdubar and Urhamsi rode in the ship,

37. where they placed them they rode.

---

38. His wife to him also said to Hasisadra afar off:

39. Izdubar goes away, he is satisfied, he performs

40. that which thou hast given him, and returns to his country.

41. And he carried the spear? of Izdubar,

42. and the ship touched the shore.

43. Hasisadra to him also said to Izdubar:

44. Izdubar thou goest away, thou art satisfied, thou performest

45. that which I have given thee, and thou re-turnest to thy country.

46. Be revealed to thee Izdubar the concealed story;

47. and the judgment of the gods be related to thee.

48. This account like bitumen . . . .

49. its renown like the Amurdin tree . . . .

50. when the account a hand shall take . . . .

51. Izdubar, this in his hearing heard, and . . . .

52. he collected great stones . . . .

COLUMN VI.

1. they dragged it and to . . . .

2. he carried the account . . . .

3. piled up the great stones . . . .

4. to his mule . . . .

---

5. Izdubar to him also said

6. to Urhamsi: this account . . . .

7. If a man in his heart take . . . .

8. may they bring him to Erech Suburi 9 speech . . . .

10. I will give an account and turn to. . . .

11. For 10 kaspu (70 miles) they journeyed the stage, for 20 kapsu (140 miles) they journeyed the stage

12. and Izdubar saw the hole . . .

13. they returned to the midst of Erech Suburi.

14. noble of men . . . .

15. in his return . . . .

16. Izdubar approached . . . .

17. and over his face coursed his tears, and he said to Urhamsi:

18. At my misfortune Urhamsi in my turning,

19. at my misfortune is my heart troubled.

20. I have not done good to my own self;

21. and the lion of the earth does good.

22. Then for 20 kaspu (140 miles) . . . .

23. . . . . then I opened . . . . the instrument

24. the sea not to its wall then could I get,

25. And they left the ship by the shore, 20 kaspu (140 miles) they journeyed the stage.

26. For 30 kaspu (210 miles) they made the ascent, they came to the midst of Erech Suburi.

---

27. Izdubar to her also said to Urhamsi the boatman:

28. Ascend Urhamsi over where the wall of Erech will go;

29. the cylinders are scattered, the bricks of its casing are not made,

30. and its foundation is not laid to thy height;

31. 1 measure the circuit of the city, 1 measure of plantations, 1 measure the boundary of the temple of Nantur the house of Ishtar,

32. 3 measures together the divisions of Erech . . .

The opening line of the next tablet is preserved, it reads: "Tammabukku in the house of the . . . . was left." After this the story is again lost for several lines, and where it reappears Izdubar is mourning for Heabani. In my first account in "Assyrian Discoveries" there are several errors which were unavoidable from the state of the twelfth tablet.

I am now able to correct some of these, and find the words tambukku and mikke do not refer to the author or manner of the death of Heabani, who most probably died in attempting to imitate the feat of Izdubar when he destroyed the lion.

The fragments of this tablet are:—

COLUMN I.

1. Tammabukku in the house of the . . . . was left

(Several lines lost.)

1. Izdubar . . . .

2. When to . . . .

3. to happiness thou . . . .

4. a cloak shining . .

5. like a misfortune also . . . .

6. The noble banquet thou dost not share,

7. to the assembly they do not call thee:

8. The bow from the ground thou dost not lift,

9. what the bow has struck escapes thee:

10. The mace in thy hand thou dost not grasp,

11. the spoil defies thee:

12. Shoes on thy feet thou dost not wear,

13. the slain on the ground thou dost not stretch.

14. Thy wife whom thou lovest thou dost not kiss,

15. thy wife whom thou hatest thou dost not strike;

16. Thy child whom thou lovest thou dost not kiss,

17. thy child whom thou hatest thou dost not strike;

18. The arms of the earth have taken thee.

19. O darkness, O darkness, mother Ninazu, O darkness.

20. Her noble stature as his mantle covers him

21. her feet like a deep well enclose him.

This is the bottom of the first column. The next column has lost all the upper part, it appears to have contained the remainder of this lament, an appeal to one of the gods on behalf of Heabani, and a repetition of the lamentation, the third person being used instead of the second. The fragments commence at the middle of this:

1. his wife whom he hated he struck,

2. his child whom he loved he kissed;

3. his child whom he hated he struck,

4. the might of the earth has taken him.

5. O darkness, O darkness, mother Ninazu, O darkness

6. Her noble stature as his mantle covers him,

7. her feet like a deep well enclose him.

8. Then Heabani from the earth

9. Simtar did not take him, Asakku did not take him, the earth took him.

10. The resting place of Nergal the unconquered did not take him, the earth took him.

11. In the place of the battle of heroes they did not strike him, the earth took him.

12. Then . . . . ni son of Ninsun for his servant Heabani wept;

13. to the house of Bel alone he went.

14. "Father Bel, a sting to the earth has struck me,

15. a deadly wound to the earth has struck me,

COLUMN III.

1. Heabani who to fly . . . .

2. Simtar did not take him . . . .

3. the resting place of Nergal the unconquered did not take him . . .

4. In the place of the battle of heroes they did not . . . .

5. Father Bel the matter do not despise . . . .

6. Father Sin, a sting . . . .

7. a deadly wound . . . .

8. Heabani who to fly . . . .

9. Simtar did not take him . . . .

10. the resting-place of Nergal . . . .

(About 12 lines lost, containing repetition of this passage.)

23. Simtar . . . .

24. the resting place of Nergal the unconquered

25. in the place of the battle of heroes they did not . . . .

26. Father Hea . . .

27. To the noble warrior Merodach . . . .

28. Noble warrior Merodach . . . .

29. the divider . . . .

30. the spirit . . . .

31. To his father . . . .

32. the noble warrior Merodach son of Hea

33. the divider the earth opened, and

34. the spirit (or ghost) of Heabani like glass (or transparent) from the earth arose:

35. . . . . . and thou explainest,

36. he pondered and repeated this:

COLUMN IV.

1. Terrible my friend, terrible my friend,

2. may the earth cover what thou hast seen, terrible,

3. I will not tell my friend, I will not tell,

4. When the earth covers what I have seen I will tell thee.

5. . . . . . . thou sittest weeping

6. . . . . . . may you sit may you weep

7. . . . . . . in youth also thy heart rejoice

8. . . . . . . become old, the worm entering

9. . . . . . . in youth also thy heart rejoice

10 full of dust

11. . . . . he passed over

12. . . . . . I see

Here there is a serious blank in the inscription, about twenty lines being lost, and I conjecturally insert a fragment which appears to belong to this part of the narrative. It is very curious from the geographical names it contains.

1. . . . . . I poured out . . . .

2. . . . . which thou trusted . . . .

3. . . . . city of Babylon *ri* . . . .

4. . . . . which he was blessed . . . .

5. . . . . may he mourn for my fault . . . .

6. . . . . may he mourn for him and for . . . .

7. . . . . Kisu and Harriskalama, may he mourn

8. . . . . his . . . . Cutha . . . .

9. . . . . Eridu? and Nipur . . . .

The rest of Column IV. is lost, and of the next column there are only remains of the two first lines.

COLUMN V.

1. like a good prince who . . . .

2. like . . . .

Here there are about thirty lines missing, the story recommencing with Column VI., which is perfect.

COLUMN VI.

1. On a couch reclining and

2. pure water drinking.

3. He who in battle is slain, thou seest and I see;

4. His father and his mother carry his head,

5. and his wife over him weeps;

6. His friends on the ground are standing,

7. thou seest and I see.

8. His spoil on the ground is uncovered,

9. of the spoil account is not taken,

10. thou seest and I see.

11. The captives conquered come after; the food

12. which in the tents is placed is eaten.

---

13. The twelfth tablet of the legends of Izdubar.

14. Like the ancient copy written and made clear. This passage closes this great national work, which even in its present mutilated form is of the greatest importance in relation to the civilization, manners, and customs of this ancient people. The main feature in this part of the Izdubar legends is the description of the Flood in the eleventh tablet, which evidently refers to the same event as the Flood of Noah in Genesis.

In my two papers in "The Transactions of the Biblical Archæological Society," vol. ii. and vol. iii. I have given some comparisons with the Biblical account and that of Berosus, and I have made similar comparisons in my work, "Assyrian Discoveries; " but I have myself to acknowledge that these comparisons are to a great extent superficial, a thorough comparison of the Biblical and Babylonian accounts of the Flood being only possible in conjunction with a critical examination both of the

Chaldean and Biblical texts. Biblical criticism is, however, a subject on which I am not competent to pronounce an independent opinion, and the views of Biblical scholars on the matter are so widely at variance, and some of them so unmistakably coloured by prejudice, that I feel I could not take up any of the prevailing views without being a party to the controversy.

There is only one point which I think should not be avoided in this matter: it is the view of a large section of scholars that the Book of Genesis contains, in some form, matter taken from two principal independent sources; one is termed the Jehovistic narrative, the other the Elohistic. The authorship and dates of the original documents and the manner, date, and extent of their combination, are points which I shall not require to notice, and I must confess I do not think we are at present in a position to form a judgment upon them. I think all will admit a connection of some sort between the Biblical narrative and those of Berosus and the cuneiform texts, but between Chaldea and Palestine was a wide extent of country inhabited by different nations, whose territories formed a connecting link between these two extremes. The Aramean and Hittite races who once inhabited the region along the Euphrates and in Syria have passed away, their history has been lost, and their mythology and traditions are unknown; until future researches on the sites of their cities shall reveal the position in which their traditions stood towards those of Babylonia and Palestine, we shall not be able to clear up the connection between the two.

There are some differences between the accounts in Genesis and the Inscriptions, but when we consider the differences between the two countries of Palestine and Babylonia these variations do not appear greater than we should expect. Chaldea was essentially a mercantile and maritime country, well watered and fiat, while Palestine was a hilly region with no great rivers, and the Jews were shut out from the coast, the maritime regions being mostly in the hands of the Philistines and Phoenicians. There was a total difference between the religious ideas of the two peoples, the Jews believing in one God, the creator and lord of the Universe, while the Babylonians worshipped gods and lords many, every city having its local deity, and these being joined by complicated relations in a poetical mythology, which was in marked contrast to the severe simplicity of the Jewish system. With such differences it was only natural that, in relating the same stories, each nation should colour them in accordance with its own ideas, and stress would naturally in each case be laid upon points with which they were familiar. Thus we should expect beforehand that there would be differences in the narrative such as we actually find, and we may also notice that the cuneiform account does not always coincide even with the account of the same events given by Berosus from Chaldean sources.

The great value of the inscriptions describing the Flood consists in the fact that they form an independent testimony in favour of the Biblical narrative at a much earlier date than any other evidence.

With reference to the size of the ark there is certainly a discrepancy, for although the Chaldean measures are effaced it is evident that in the inscription the breadth and height of the vessel are stated to be the same, while these are given in Genesis as fifty cubits and thirty cubits respectively.

With regard to those who were saved in the ark there is again a clear difference between the two accounts, the Bible stating that only eight persons, all of the family of Noah, were saved, while the inscription includes his servants, friends, and boatmen or pilots; but certainly the most remarkable difference between the two is with respect to the duration of the deluge. On this point the inscription gives seven days for the flood, and seven days for the resting of the ark on the mountain, while the Bible gives the commencement of the flood on the 17th day of the second month and its termination on the 27th day of the second month in the following year, making a total duration of one year and ten days. Here it may be remarked, that those scholars who believe in two distinct documents being included in Genesis, hold that in the Jehovistic narrative the statement is that the flood lasted forty days, which is certainly nearer to the time specified in the cuneiform text. Forty is, however, often an ambiguous word, meaning "many," and not necessarily fixing exactly the number. There is again a difference as to the mountain on which the ark rested; Nizir, the place mentioned in the cuneiform text, being east of Assyria, probably between latitudes 35° and 36° (see "Assyrian Discoveries," pp. 216, 217), while Ararat, the mountain mentioned in the Bible, was north of Assyria, near Lake Van. It is evident that different traditions have placed the mountain of the ark in totally different positions, and there is not positive proof as to which is the earlier traditionary spot. The word Ararat is derived from an old Babylonian word *Urdu*, meaning "highland," and might be a general term for any hilly country, and I think it quite possible that when Genesis was written the land of Armenia was not intended by this term. My own view is that the more southern part of the mountains east of Assyria was the region of the original tradition, and that the other sites are subsequent identifications due to changes in geographical names and other causes.

In the account of sending forth the birds there is a difference in detail between the Bible and the Inscriptions which cannot be explained away; this and other similar differences will serve to show that neither of the two documents is copied directly from the other.

Some of the other differences are evidently due to the opposite religious systems of the two countries, but there is again a curious point in connection with the close of the Chaldean legend, this is the translation of the hero of the Flood.

In the Book of Genesis it is not Noah but the seventh patriarch Enoch who is translated, three generations before the Flood.

There appears to have been some connection or confusion between Enoch and Noah in ancient tradition; both are holy men, and Enoch is said, like Noah, to have predicted the Flood.

It is a curious fact that the dynasty of gods, with which Egyptian mythical history commences, shows some similar points.

This dynasty has sometimes seven, sometimes ten reigns, and in the Turin Papyrus of kings, which gives ten reigns, there is the same name for the seventh and tenth reign, both being called Horus, and the seventh reign is stated at 300 years, which is the length of life of the seventh patriarch Enoch after the birth of his son.

I here show the three lists, the Egyptian gods, the Jewish patriarchs, and Chaldean kings.

Egypt.
Ptah.
Ra.
Su.
Seb.
Hosiri.
Set.
Hor.
Tut
Ma.
Hor.

Jewish Patriarchs.
Adam.

Seth.
Enos.
Cainan.
Mahalaleel
Jared.
Enoch.
Methusaleh.
Lamech.
Noah.

Chaldean Kings.
Alorus.
Alaparus.
Almelon.
Ammenon.
Amegalarus.
Daonus.
Ædorachus.
Amempsin.
Otiartes.
Xisuthrus.

I think it cannot be accidental that in each case we have ten names, but on the other hand there is no resemblance between the names, which appear to be independent in origin. What connection there may be between the three lists we have at present no means of knowing. It is probable that the literature of the old Syrian peoples, if it should ever be recovered, may help us to the discovery of the connection between these various accounts.

The seal discussed in p. 106, belonged to a Syrian chief in the ninth century B.C., and the devices upon it, the sacred tree, and composite beings, show similar stories and ideas to have prevailed there to those in Babylonia.

One question which will be asked, and asked in vain is: "Did either of the two races, Jews or Babylonians, borrow from the other the traditions of these early times, and if so, when?"

There is one point in connection with this question worth noticing: these traditions are not fixed to any localities near Palestine, but are, even on the showing of the Jews themselves, fixed to the neighbourhood of the

Euphrates valley, and Babylonia in particular; this of course is clearly stated in the Babylonian inscriptions and traditions.

Eden, according even to the Jews, was by the Euphrates and Tigris; the cities of Babylon, Larancha, and Sippara were supposed to have been founded before the Flood. Surippak was the city of the ark, the mountains east of the Tigris were the resting-place of the ark, Babylon was the site of the tower, and Ur of the Chaldees the birthplace of Abraham. These facts and the further statement that Abraham, the father and first leader of the Hebrew race, migrated from Ur to Harran in Syria, and from there to Palestine, are all so much evidence in favour of the hypothesis that Chaldea was the original home of these stories, and that the Jews received them originally from the Babylonians; but on the other hand there are such striking differences in some parts of the legends, particularly in the names of the patriarchs before the Flood, that it is evident further information is required before attempting to decide, the question. Passing to the next, the twelfth and last tablet, the picture there given, the lament for Heabani, and the curious story of his ghost rising from the ground at the bidding of Merodach, serve to make this as important in relation to the Babylonian religion as the eleventh tablet was to the book of Genesis.

Asakku is the spirit of one of the diseases, and Simtar is the attendant of the goddess of Hades; the trouble appears to be that Simtar and Asakku would not receive the soul of Heabani, while he was equally repudiated by Nergal and shut out from the region appointed for warlike heroes. The soul of Heabani was confined to the earth, and, not resting there, intercession was made to transfer him to the region of the blessed. I at one time added to this tablet a fragment which then appeared to belong and which I interpreted to refer to Heabani's dwelling in hell and taking his way from there to heaven. The discovery of a new fragment has forced me to alter both the translation and position of this notice, which I now place in the seventh tablet. This considerably weakens my argument that the Babylonians had two separate regions for a future state, one of bliss, the other of joy.

Under the fourth column I have provisionally placed a curious fragment where Izdubar appears to call on his cities to mourn with him for his friend. This tablet is remarkable for the number of cities mentioned as already existing in the time of Izdubar. Combining this notice with other parts of the legends, the statements of Berosus and the notice of the cities of Nimrod in Genesis, we get the following list of the oldest known cities in the Euphrates valley.

1. Babylon.
2. Borsippa.
3. Cutha.
4. Larancha.
5. Surippak.
6. Eridu.
7. Nipur.
8. Erech.
9. Akkad.
10. Calneh.
11. Sippara.
12. Kisu.
13. Harriskalama.
14. Ganganna.
15. Amarda.
16. Assur.
17. Nineveh.
18. Rehobothair.
19. Resen.
20. Calah.

So far as the various statements go, all these cities and probably many others were in existence in the time of Nimrod, and some of them even before the Flood; the fact, that the Babylonians four thousand years ago believed their cities to be of such antiquity, shows that they were not recent foundations, and their attainments at that time in the arts and sciences proves that their civilization had already known ages of progress. The epoch of Izdubar must be considered at present as the commencement of the united monarchy in Babylonia, and as marking the first of the series of great conquests in Western Asia, but how far back we have to go from our earliest known monuments to reach his era we cannot now tell.

It is probable that after the death of Izdubar the empire he had founded fell to pieces, and was only partially restored when Urukh, king of Ur, extended his power over the country and founded the Chaldean or Southern Sumerian dynasty.

Every nation has its hero, and it was only natural on the revival of his empire that the Babylonians should consecrate the memory of the king, who had first aimed to give them that unity without which they were powerless as a nation.

CHAPTER XVII: CONCLUSION.

Notices of Genesis.—Correspondence of names.—Abram.—Ur of Chaldees.—Ishmael.—Sargon.—His birth.—Concealed in ark.—Age of Nimrod.—Doubtful theories.—Creation.—Garden of Eden.— Oannes.—Berosus.—Izdubar legends.—Urukh of Ur.—Babylonian seals.—Egyptian names.—Assyrian sculptures.

SCATTERED through various cuneiform inscriptions are other notices, names, or passages, connected with the Book of Genesis. Although the names of the Genesis patriarchs are not in the inscriptions giving the history of the mythical period, the corresponding personages being, as I have shown (p. 290), all under different names, yet some of these Genesis patriarchal names are found detached in the inscriptions.

The name Adam is in the Creation legends, but only in a general sense as man, not as a proper name. Several of the other names of antediluvian patriarchs correspond with Babylonian words and roots, such as Cain with gina and kinu, to "stand upright," to be "right," Enoch with Emuk or Enuk, "wise," and Noah with nuh, "rest," or "satisfaction;" but beyond these some of the names appear as proper names also in Babylonia, and among these are Cainan, Lamech, and Tubal Cain.

Cainan is found as the name of a Babylonian town Kan-nan; the meaning may be "fish canal," its people were- sometimes called Kanunai or Canaanites, the same name as that of the original inhabitants of Palestine. In early times tribes often migrated and carried their geographical names to their new homes; it is possible that there was some connection of this sort between the two Canaans.

Lamech has already been pointed out by Palmer ("Egyptian Chronicles," vol. i. p. 56), in the name of the Deified Phoenician patriarch Diamich; this name is found in the cuneiform texts as Dumugu and Lamga, two forms of a name of the moon.

Tubal Cain, the father or instructor of all metal workers, has been compared with the name of Vulcan, the god of smiths, the two certainly corresponding both in name and character. The corresponding deity in Babylonian mythology, the god of fire, melter of metals, &c., has a name formed of two characters which read Bil-kan.

Some of the names of patriarchs after the Flood are found as names of towns in Syria, but not in Babylonia; among these are Reu or Ragu, Serug, and Harran.

The name of Abramu or Abram, called no doubt after the father of the faithful, is found in the Assyrian inscriptions in the time of Esarhaddon. After the captivity of the ten tribes, some of the Israelites prospered in Assyria, and rose to positions of trust in the empire. Abram was one of these, he was sukulu rabu or "great attendant" of Esarhaddon, and was eponym in Assyria, B.C. 677. Various other Hebrew names are found in Assyria about this time, including Pekah, Hoshea, and several compounded with the two Divine names Elohim and Jehovah, showing that both these names were in use among the Israelites. The presence of proper names founded on the Genesis stories, like Abram, and the use at this time of these forms of the Divine name, should be taken into consideration in discussing the evidence of the antiquity of Genesis.

It is a curious fact that the rise of the kingdom of Ur (cir. B.C. 2000 to 1850) coincides with the date generally given for the life of Abraham, who is stated (Genesis xi. 31) to have come out of Ur of the Chaldees, by which title I have no doubt the Babylonian city of Ur is meant. There is not the slightest evidence of a northern Ur and a northern land o the Chaldees at this period.

Some of the other Genesis names are found very much earlier, the first which appears on a contemporary monument being Ishmael. In the reign of Hammurabi, king of Babylonia, about B.C. 1550, among the witnesses to some documents at Larsa in Babylonia, appears a man named "Abuha son of Ishmael." This period in Babylonia is supposed to have been one of foreign and Arabian dominion, and other Hittite and Arabian names are found in the inscriptions of the time.

In the Babylonian records we might expect to find some notice of the wars of Chedorlaomer, king of Elam, mentioned in Genesis xiv. Now although evidence has been found confirming the existence of a powerful monarchy in Elam at this age, and satisfactory proof of the correctness of the proper names mentioned in this chapter, no direct record of these conquests has been discovered, but we must remember that our knowledge of Babylonian history is yet in its infancy, and even the outlines of the chronology are unknown.

After the time of Abraham the book of Genesis is concerned with the affairs of Palestine, and of the countries in its immediate vicinity, and it has no connection with Babylonian history and traditions; there remains, however, one story which has a striking likeness to that of Moses in the ark, and which, although not within the period covered by Genesis, is of great interest in connection with the early history of the Jews.

Sargina or Sargon I. was a Babylonian monarch who reigned at the city of Akkad about B.C. 1600. The name of Sargon signifies the right, true, or legitimate king, and may have been assumed on his ascending the throne. Sargon was probably of obscure origin, and desiring to strengthen his claim to the throne put out the story given in this tablet to connect himself with the old line of kings. This curious story is found on fragments of tablets from Kouyunjik, and reads as follows:

1. Sargina the powerful king the king of Akkad am I.

2. My mother was a princess, my father I did not know, a brother of my father ruled over the country.

3. In the city of Azupiranu which by the side of the river Euphrates is situated

4. my mother the princess conceived me; in difficulty she brought me forth

5. She placed me in an ark of rushes, with bitumen my exit she sealed up.

6. She launched me on the river which did not drown me.

7. The river carried me, to Akki the water carrier it brought me.

8. Akki the water carrier in tenderness of bowels lifted me;

9. Akki the water carrier as his child brought me up,

10. Akki the water carrier as his husbandman placed me,

11. and in my husbandry Ishtar prospered me.

12. 45? years the kingdom I have ruled,

13. the people of the dark races I governed,

14. . . . . over rugged countries with chariots of bronze I rode,

15. I govern the upper countries

16. I rule? over the chiefs of the lower countries

17. To the sea coast three times I advanced, Dilmun submitted,

18. Durankigal bowed, &c. &c.

After this follows an address to any king who should at a later time notice the inscription.

This story is supposed to have happened about B.C. 1600, rather earlier than the supposed age of Moses; and, as we know that the fame of Sargon reached Egypt, it is quite likely that this account had a connection with the events related in Exodus ii., for every action, when once performed, has a tendency to be repeated.

In the body of my present work I have given the various fragments of the Legends describing the Creation, Flood, time of Nimrod, &c.; and I have

indicated, as well as I can at present, the grounds for my present conclusions respecting them, and what are their principal points of contact with the Bible narrative of Genesis.

I have also put forward some theories to account for various difficulties in the stories, and to connect together the fragmentary accounts.

The most hazardous of these theories is the one which makes Izdubar or Nimrod reign in the middle of the twenty-third century before the Christian era. I have founded this theory on several plausible, but probably merely superficial grounds; and if any one accepts my view on this point, it will be only for similar reasons to those which caused me to propose it; namely, because, failing this, we have no clue whatever to the age and position of the most famous hero in Oriental tradition.

I never lose sight myself of the fact, that apart from the more perfect and main parts of these texts, both in the decipherment of the broken fragments and in the various theories I have projected respecting them, I have changed my own opinions many times, and I have no doubt that any accession of new material would change again my views respecting the parts affected by it. These theories and conclusions, however, although not always correct, have, on their way, assisted the inquiry, and have led to the more accurate knowledge of the texts; for certainly in cuneiform matters we have often had to advance through error to truth.

In my theory for the position of Nimrod, one thing is certainly clear: I have placed him as low in the chronology as it is possible to make him.

Making the date of Nimrod so recent as B.C. 2250, I have only left from 200 to 250 years between his time and the age of the oldest known monuments. Looking at the fact that it is highly probable that these legends were written about B.C. 2000, the intervening period of two centuries does not appear too great. I think it probable that the traditions on which these legends were founded arose shortly after the death of Izdubar; in fact, I think that every tradition which has any foundation in fact springs up within a generation of the time when the circumstances happened. With regard to the supernatural element introduced into the story, it is similar in nature to many such additions to historical narratives, especially in the East; but I would not reject those events which may have happened, because in order to illustrate a current belief; or add to the romance of the story, the writer has introduced the supernatural.

There is, I think, now too general a tendency to repudiate the earlier part of history, because of its evident inaccuracies and the marvellous element generally combined with it. The early poems and stories of almost every nation are, by some writers, resolved into elaborate descriptions of natural phenomena; and in some cases, if this were true, the myth would have taken to create it a genius as great as that of the philosophers who explain it.

The stories and myths given in the foregoing pages have, probably, very different values; some are genuine traditions—some compiled to account for natural phenomena, and some pure romances. At the head of their history and traditions the Babylonians placed an account of the creation of the world; and, although different forms of this story were current, in certain features they all agreed. Beside the account of the present animals, they related the creation of legions of monster forms which disappeared before the human epoch, and they accounted for the great problem of humanity—the presence of evil in the world—by making out that it proceeded from the original chaos, the spirit of confusion and darkness, which was the origin of all things, and which was even older than the gods.

The principal Babylonian story of the Creation, given in Chapter V., substantially agrees, as far as it is preserved, with the Biblical account. According to it, there was a chaos of watery matter before the Creation, and from this all things were generated.

We have then a considerable blank, the contents of which we can only conjecture, and after this we come to the creation of the heavenly orbs.

The fifth tablet in the series relates how God created the constellations of the stars, the signs of the zodiac, the planets or wandering stars, the moon and tine sun. After another blank we have a fragment, the first I recognized which relates the creation of wild and domestic animals; it is curious here that the original taming of domestic animals was even then so far back that all knowledge of it was lost, and the "animals of the city," or domestic animals, were considered different creations to the "animals of the desert," or wild animals.

Our next fragments refer to the creation of mankind, called Adam, as in the Bible; he is made perfect, and instructed in his various religious duties, but afterwards he joins with the dragon of the deep, the animal of Tiamat, the spirit of chaos, and offends against his god, who curses him, and calls down on his head all the evils and troubles of humanity.

This is followed by a war between the dragon and powers of evil, or chaos on one side and the gods on the other. The gods have weapons forged for them, and Merodach undertakes to lead the heavenly host against the dragon. The war, which is described with spirit, ends of course in the triumph of the principles of good, and so far as I know the Creation tablets end here.

In Chapter V. I have given as far as possible translations and comments on these texts, and to meet the requirements of those who desire to study them in the cuneiform character I have arranged to publish copies of the principal fragments of the Creation tablets in the "Transactions of the Society of Biblical Archæology."

The fragments I have selected for this purpose are:—

I. Fragment of the first tablet, describing the chaos at the beginning of the world.

II. Fragment of the fifth tablet, describing the creation of the heavenly bodies.

III. Obverse and reverse of the tablet, describing the fall of man.

IV. Obverse and reverse of the principal fragment, describing the conflict between the gods and the spirit of chaos.

Besides this account of the Creation I have given other fragments bearing upon the same events, these differing considerably from the longer account. The principal feature in the second account is the description of the eagle-headed men with their family of leaders—this legend clearly showing the origin of the eagle-headed figures represented on the Assyrian sculptures.

It is probable that some of these Babylonian legends contained detailed descriptions of the Garden of Eden, which was most likely the district of Karduniyas, as Sir Henry Rawlinson believes.

There are coincidences in respect to the geography of the region and its name which render the identification very probable; the four rivers in each case, two, the Euphrates and Tigris, certainly identical, the known fertility of the region, its name, sometimes Gan-dunu, so similar to Gan-eden (the Garden of Eden), and other considerations, all tend towards the view that it is the Paradise of Genesis.

There are evidences of the belief in the tree of life, which is one of the most common emblems on the seals and larger sculptures, and is even used as an ornament on dresses; a sacred tree is also several times mentioned in these legends, but at present there is no direct connection known between the tree and the Fall, although the gem engravings render it very probable that there was a legend of this kind like the one in Genesis.

In the history of Berosus mention is made of a composite being, half man, half fish, named Oannes, who was supposed to have appeared out of the sea and to have taught to the Babylonians all their learning. The Babylonian and Assyrian sculptures have made us familiar with the figure of Oannes, and have so far given evidence that Berosus has truly described this mythological figure, but it is a curious fact that the legend of Oannes, which must have been one of the Babylonian stories of the Creation, has not yet been recovered.

Besides this, there are evidently many stories of early times still unknown, or only known by mere fragments or allusions.

The fables which I have given in Chapter IX. form a series now appearing to be separate from the others, and my only excuse for inserting them here was my desire to exhibit as clearly and fully as possible the literature of the great epoch which produced the Genesis tablets.

Most of the other stories, so far as I can judge, are fixed to the great period before the Flood, when celestial visitors came backwards and forwards to the earth, and the inhabitants of the world were very clearly divided into the good and bad, but the stories are only fables with a moral attached, and have little connection with Babylonian history.

Two of these stories are very curious, and may hereafter turn out of great importance; one is the story of the sin committed by the god Zu, and the other the story of Atarpi.

Berosus in his history has given an account of ten Chaldean kings who reigned before the Flood, and the close of this period is well known from the descriptions of the Deluge in the Bible, the Deluge tablet, and the work of Berosus. According to Berosus several of the Babylonian cities were built before the Flood, and various arts were known, including writing. The enormous reigns given by Berosus to his ten kings, making a total of 432,000 years, force us to discard the idea that the details are historical, although there may be some foundation for his statement of a civilization before the Deluge. The details given in the inscriptions describing the Flood leave no doubt that both the Bible and the Babylonian story describe the same event, and the Flood becomes the starting point for the modern world in both histories. According to Berosus 86 kings reigned for 34,080 years after the Flood down to the Median conquest. If these kings are historical, it is doubtful if they formed a continuous line, and they could scarcely cover a longer period than 1,000 years. The Median or Elamite conquest took place about B.C. 2450, and, if we allow the round number 1,000 years for the previous period, it will make the Flood fall about B.C. 3500. In a fragmentary inscription with a list of Babylonian kings, some names are given which appear to belong to the 86 kings of Berosus, but our information about this period is so scanty that nothing can be said about this dynasty, and a suggestion as to the date of the Deluge must be received with more than the usual grain of salt.

We can see, however, that there was a civilized race in Babylonia before the Median Conquest, the progress of which must have received a rude shock when the country was overrun by the uncivilized Eastern borderers.

Among the fragmentary notices of this period is the portion of the inscription describing the building of the Tower of Babel and the dispersion, unfortunately too mutilated to make much use of it.

It is probable from the fragments of Berosus that the incursions and dominion of the Elamites lasted about two hundred years, during which the country suffered very much from them.

I think it probable that Izdubar, or Nimrod, owed a great portion of his fame in the first instance to his slaying Humbaba, and that he readily found the means of uniting the country under one sceptre, as the people saw the evils of disunion, which weakened them and laid them open to foreign invasion.

The legends of Izdubar or Nimrod commence with a description of the evils brought upon Babylonia by foreign invasion, the conquest and sacking of the city of Erech being one of the incidents in the story. Izdubar, a famous hunter, who claimed descent from a long line of kings, reaching up to the time of the Flood, now comes forward; he has a dream, and after much trouble a hermit named Heabani is persuaded by Zaidu, a hunter, and two females, to come to Erech and interpret the dream of Izdubar. Heabani, having heard the fame of Izdubar, brings to Erech a midannu or tiger to test his strength, and Izdubar slays it. After these things, Izdubar and Heabani become friends, and, having invoked the gods, they start to attack Humbaba, an Elamite, who tyrannized over Babylonia. Humbaba dwelt in a thick forest, surrounded by a wall, and here he was visited by the two friends, who slew him and carried off his regalia.

Izdubar was now proclaimed king, and extended his authority from the Persian Gulf to the Armenian mountains, his court and palace being at Erech. Ishtar, called Nana and Uzur-amatsa, the daughter according to some authorities of Anu, according to others of Elu or Bel, and according to others of Sin, the moon god, was widow of Dumuzi, a *rihu* or ruler. She was queen and goddess of Erech, and fell in love with Izdubar, offering him her hand and kingdom. He refused, and the goddess, angry at his answer, ascended to heaven and petitioned her father Anu to create a bull for her, to be an instrument of her vengeance against Izdubar. Anu complied, and created the bull, on which Izdubar and Heabani collected a band of warriors and went against it. Heabani took hold of the animal by its head and tail, while Izdubar slew it.

Ishtar on this cursed Izdubar, and descended to Hell or Hades to attempt once more to summon unearthly powers against Izdubar. She descends to the infernal regions, which are vividly described, and, passing through its seven gates, is ushered into the presence of the queen of the dead. The world of love goes wrong in the absence of Ishtar, and on the petition of the gods she is once more brought to the earth, ultimately Anatu, her mother, satisfying her vengeance by striking Izdubar with a loathsome disease.

Heabani, the friend of Izdubar, is now killed, and Izdubar, mourning his double affliction, abandons his kingdom and wanders into the desert to seek the advice of Hasisadra his ancestor, who had been translated for his piety and now dwelt with the gods.

Izdubar now had a dream, and after this wandered to the region where gigantic composite monsters held and controlled the rising and setting sun, from these learned the road to the region of the blessed, and, passing across a great waste of sand, he arrived at a region where splendid trees were laden with jewels instead of fruit.

Izdubar then met two females, named Siduri and Sabitu, after an adventure with whom he found a boatman named Ur-hamsi, who undertook to navigate him to the region of Hasisadra.

Coining near the dwelling of the blessed, he found it surrounded by the waters of death, which he had to cross in order to reach the region.

On arriving at the other side, Izdubar was met by one Ragmu, who engaged him in conversation about Heabani, and then Hasisadra, taking up the conversation, described to him the Deluge. Izdubar was afterwards cured of his illness and returned with Urhamsi to Erech, where he mourned anew for his friend Heabani, and on intercession with the gods the ghost of Heabani arises from the ground where the body had lain.

The details of this story, and especially the accounts of the regions inhabited by the dead, are very striking, and illustrate, in a wonderful manner, the religious views of the people.

It is probable that Izdubar was, as I have already stated, Nimrod, and that he commenced his life as a hunter, afterwards delivering his country from foreign dominion, and slaying the usurper.

He then extended his empire into Assyria, which he colonized, and founded Nineveh. The empire founded by Nimrod probably fell to pieces at his death; but the Assyrian colonies grew into a powerful state, and after a brief period, Babylonia revived under Urukh, king of Ur, with whom commenced the monumental era.

Here the legendary and traditional age ends, and about this time the stories appear to have been committed to writing.

It is worth while here to pause, and consider the evidence of the existence of these legends from this time down to the seventh century B.C.

We have first the seals: of these there are some hundreds in European museums, and among the earliest are many specimens carved with scenes from the Genesis legends; some of these are probably older than B.C. 2000, others may be ranged at various dates down to B.C. 1500.

After B.C. 1500, the literature of Babylonia is unknown, and we lose sight of all evidence of these legends for some centuries. In the meantime Egypt supplies a few notices bearing on the subject, which serve to show that knowledge of them was still kept up. Nearly thirteen hundred years before the Christian era one of the Egyptian poems likens a hero to the Assyrian chief, Kazartu, a great hunter. Kazartu probably means a "strong," "powerful," one, and it has already been suggested that the reference here is to the fame of Nimrod. A little later, in the period B.C. 1100 to 800, we have in Egypt many persons named after Nimrod, showing a knowledge of the mighty hunter there.

On the revival of the Assyrian empire, about B.C. 990, we come again to numerous references to the Genesis legends, and these continue through almost every reign down to the close of the empire. The Assyrians carved the sacred tree and cherubims on their walls, they depicted in the temples the struggle between Merodach and the dragon, the figure of Oannes and the eagle-headed man, they decorated their portals with figures of Nimrod strangling a lion, and carved the struggles of Nimrod and Heabani with the lion and the bull even on their stone vases.

Just as the sculptures of the Greek temples, the paintings on the vases and the carving on their gems were taken from their myths and legends, so the series of myths and legends belonging to the valley of the Euphrates furnished materials for the sculptor, the engraver, and the painter, among the ancient Babylonians and Assyrians.

In this way we have continued evidence of the existence of these legends down to the time of Assurbanipal, B.C. 673 to 626, who caused the present known copies to be made for his library at Nineveh.

Search in Babylonia would, no doubt, yield much earlier copies of all these works, but that search has not yet been instituted, and for the present we have to be contented with our Assyrian copies. Looking, however, at the world-wide interest of the subjects, and at the important evidence which perfect copies of these works would undoubtedly give, there can be no doubt that the subject of further search and discovery will not slumber, and that all I have here written will one day be superseded by newer texts and fuller and more perfect light.

A NOTE TO THE READER

WE HOPED YOU LOVED THIS BOOK. IF YOU DID, PLEASE LEAVE A REVIEW ON AMAZON TO LET EVERYONE ELSE KNOW WHAT YOU THOUGHT.

WE WOULD ALSO LIKE TO THANK OUR SPONSORS **WWW.DIGITALHISTORYBOOKS.COM** WHO MADE THE PUBLICATION OF THIS BOOK POSSIBLE.

WWW.DIGITALHISTORYBOOKS.COM PROVIDES A WEEKLY NEWSLETTER OF THE BEST DEALS IN HISTORY AND HISTORICAL FICTION.

SIGN UP TO THEIR NEWLSETTER TO FIND OUT MORE ABOUT THEIR LATEST DEALS.

Made in the USA
Las Vegas, NV
10 February 2023

67257155R00113